CONTEMPORARY SOUTHWEST

THE CAFÉ TERRA COTTA COOKBOOK

CONTEMPORARY SOUTHWEST
THE CAFÉ TERRA COTTA COOKBOOK

BY DONNA NORDIN

PHOTOGRAPHY BY

WILLIAM MCKELLAR

AN ASTOLAT BOOK

HARLOW & RATNER

EMERYVILLE, CALIFORNIA

Book Design and Illustration: McClain Design
Food Styling: Marcos Barreto
Typography: Scott Hammond
Special Thanks to: Rochelle K, Mark Economou, Andrew Luria
Props for Photography: The Kaibab Shops, Tucson, AZ
Two Plates Full, Scottsdale, AZ
Krzyzanowski & Co., Florists, Tucson, AZ

Library of Congress Cataloging-in-Publication Data

Nordin, Donna.
Contemporary southwest : the Café Terra Cotta cookbook / by Donna
Nordin ; photography by William McKellar ; illustrated by Daniel McClain.
        p.   cm.
"An Astolat book."
Includes bibliographical references and index.
ISBN 0-9627345-8-6 : $26.95
1. Cookery, American—Southwestern style. 2. Café Terra Cotta. I. Title.
TX715.2.S69N67 1995
641.5979—dc20   94-37365
                                                          CIP

Printed in Hong Kong
10 9 8 7 6 5 4 3 2 1

Harlow & Ratner
5749 Landregan Street
Emeryville, California 94608

THIS COOKBOOK
IS DEDICATED TO
MY THREE GRANDDAUGHTERS:
RYAN, CASEY, AND HUNTER.
I HOPE THE BOOK
GIVES THEM AS MUCH PLEASURE
AS THEY HAVE
GIVEN ME!

ACKNOWLEDGEMENTS

L ove of cooking usually begins at an early age and usually comes from either family or eating-out experiences. I was very lucky that my mother, Lorene Barker, and her mother, Gussie, were both good Southern cooks and exposed me to both tasteful food and sound cooking techniques. Without their influence and my mother's continuous support, my life might have taken a different direction and this book might be on auto mechanics.

After I had the cooking bug and returned to San Francisco from my educational sojourns in France, I was fortunate to meet many established and rising stars in the culinary arts in the Bay Area, including Joyce Goldstein, Jack Lirio, Marion Cunningham, and Mark Miller. When I opened my cooking school in San Francisco, I was able to book such notables as Giuliano Bugialli, Diana Kennedy, Anne Willan, John Clancy, Flo Braker (my dessert idol), and Paula Wolfert. All their talents encouraged me in my pursuit of the culinary arts.

During this time I developed close friendships with two Bay Area "foodies," Joyce Jue and Marge Poore. Their friendship and support, and the fact that they published cookbooks before me, gave me both encouragement and incentive. Their friendship will always be there, and they can feel free to publish as many books as they want. I will not attempt to keep up with them, and they can seek satisfaction that this is the only Donna Nordin cookbook where they will see their names acknowledged.

This book would not have been possible without the efforts, creativity, and dedication of our chefs and staff at Café Terra Cotta: Jeff Azersky, Marianne Banes, Steve Critcher, and Marcos Barreto in Tucson, and Matthew Lash and Charleen Badman in Scottsdale. Unfortunately, the supporting staff is too numerous to name here, but they are not nameless to me.

Converting recipes from feeding 100 to feeding four is not easy or simple. My recipe tester Yvonne Zundel, supported by Jeff Blackburn, helped immeasurably and provided security that these recipes work for the home cook in a home kitchen.

People have encouraged and cajoled me for years to write a cookbook. I dragged my feet as long as I could until Jay Harlow and Elaine Ratner pushed me over the edge, while at the same time giving me a comfort level where I could "just do it." Without Jay and Elaine this book would just be a pile of papers under my desk.

I must freely admit that I suffered through every element of this book, from selecting recipes to the endless rewrites. However, one person suffered even more — my husband and partner for life, Don Luria. He put up with the silent and audible screams, the temper tantrums, and the moods. I know that without him and his support this book would be shredded papers under Jay Harlow's desk.

CONTENTS

INTRODUCTION

~~~~~~~~

As is very common with today's chefs, my path to becoming an executive chef/ restaurant owner/advocate of contemporary southwestern cuisine was full of curves, sharp turns, and unforeseen events. As a child, I was raised in San Diego. My introduction to flavorful, spicy food was the "border" Mexican or "Cal-Mex" cuisine which was spreading north from Tijuana through southern California. My early trips to Tijuana as a teenager, often without my parents' knowledge, taught me to appreciate those distinct flavors and ingredients, which were not to be found in the mainstream restaurants where most parents took their children. My parents, however, loved Mexican food, and between Tijuana and family outings, I fell in love with chiles. Many people don't become compulsive about spicy food until later in life. In my case, however, I loved and appreciated these taste sensations very early and they have never left me.

As I grew older, went to college, and began to travel, I also realized that the border interpretation of Mexican food only touched the tip of the iceberg. Compared to the Mexican *cuisine* of the Yucatán, central Mexico, and Oaxaca, border food is merely Mexican *cooking*. As my food interest grew, my taste buds remained Mexican, but I knew the roots of cooking lay across the Atlantic in France.

My love of cooking, any cooking, became serious after I graduated from San Diego State. I moved to San Francisco. It was the mid-60s,

and San Francisco was already a restaurant town. It was easy to become even more enamored with food. As my passion for food heated up, my first marriage cooled down. When we parted ways, I kept the kitchen equipment and his name. Before long, my love of food led me to Paris where I attended Le Cordon Bleu. It was at Le Cordon Bleu that I first met Marion Cunningham, whose work I have always admired and whose friendship I have valued. I returned to France several times and completed the intensive pastry class at Le Nôtre and fell in love again. This time it was chocolate, but I didn't change my name.

Feeling comfortable with having mastered (more or less) basic French cuisine and techniques, I started to teach cooking in my home. I concentrated primarily on French cuisine and desserts (chocolate, of course). When my classes outgrew my home kitchen, I started my own cooking school along with, as a necessary evil, a cookware store in the Marina district of San Francisco. I called it La Grande Bouffe.

I had married again, a Frenchman, of course. I hated the retail side of the business, but loved the teaching side. Perhaps the most valuable part of teaching for me was meeting and becoming acquainted with and working with some true international masters including Jacques Pepin, Giuliano Bugialli, Juila Child, Diana Kennedy, and James Beard. I also became active among the foodies in San Francisco and was one of the founders of the San Francisco Professional Food Society (SFPFS). At this time, except for my friendship with Marge Poore, who teaches Mexican cuisine, the food of Mexico took a back seat in my life. Frankly, the thought of opening a restaurant never entered my mind. After all, I was still a rational person.

My pragmatism led me to make two decisions that would have a profound effect on the direction of my life. I separated from my second husband and closed the school and retail business and took to the road, teaching here and there in the San Francisco Bay Area with occasional teaching trips to the Midwest. While I was looking for more places to teach, my Chinese cooking buddy Joyce Jue suggested a cooking school in Tucson, Arizona. I wrote a letter to the owner asking if he would be interested in my teaching either French or dessert classes. I received a positive reply and was scheduled to teach five dessert classes and one French class. Fortunately for me, French cuisine was not as hot an item in Tucson as was the weather, and my French class was canceled. Since my plane to Kansas City didn't leave until the day after, the owner of the school, Donald Luria, was obligated to show me the sights of Tucson.

Between a visit to the Arizona-Sonora Desert Museum, lunch, and dinner, lightning struck. The next thing I knew, I was spending more and more time in Tucson eating Mexican cuisine while Don, a relocated Easterner sweating from the chiles, was spending more and more time figuring out how to keep me in Tucson. Finally he set the trap — "Let's open a restaurant." He was smart. After all, everyone knows a restaurant is a 24-hour-a-day job. Love blinds the eye and fogs the brain. Or was it the heat? ("So what if it's 110° in the shade?" he said. "It's a dry heat.") I said yes to a restaurant.

But what kind of restaurant? Actually it was an easy and natural decision, based on my skills and my taste preferences. The menu would have to combine my classical French training and my love for the spicy, robust flavors of Mexico, many of whose products passed through Tucson on their way to other cities. Having lived and taught in California during the time that a new California cuisine was emerging and maturing, I knew that techniques and ingredients from different parts of the world could come together in a way that would outlast fads.

Two marriages were in the making — mine to Don and ours to our vision of "Contemporary Southwestern Cuisine." Café Terra Cotta was soon to be born and I was taking what I hope will be my last husband. Our "family" has since grown to include a second Café Terra Cotta in Scottsdale. In this book you will find a collection of the menu standards and daily specials that our customers have enjoyed through the years. I hope you enjoy them, and that they inspire your own exploration of flavorful, colorful, contemporary southwestern cuisine.

DONNA NORDIN
Tucson, September 1994

THE BASICS

CONTEMPORARY
SOUTHWESTERN CUISINE

INGREDIENTS:
THE BUILDING BLOCKS
OF SOUTHWESTERN CUISINE

COOKING EQUIPMENT
AND TECHNIQUES

NOTES TO THE COOK

MENU PLANNING

WINES WITH
SOUTHWESTERN CUISINE

CONTEMPORARY SOUTHWESTERN CUISINE

〰〰〰〰〰〰

Cuisines that are based in a nation, state, or province, such as Italian, French, or Cantonese, are often easily defined. Regional cuisines, especially those with less distinct boundaries such as "southern" and "southwestern," present a more difficult problem. Their boundaries are not clear, their history is not always well documented, and as beauty is in the eye of the beholder, so the cuisine is from the view of the practitioner and the consumer.

At Café Terra Cotta we call what we serve "Contemporary Southwestern Cuisine." This phrase has been a part of our restaurant philosophy and our concept from the day in 1986 that we decided to open a restaurant. I was amazed that I was not aware of a single restaurant in Arizona that I would define as southwestern. There were Mexican restaurants galore, mostly of the "Tex-Mex" variety (tacos and enchiladas), and plenty of cowboy-style "western" steak houses (you know, the kind that cut your tie off if you make the mistake of overdressing). There were a few restaurants that were serving "nouvelle American cuisine" that now have moved in the direction of southwestern cuisine. But there was nothing that matched the image of contemporary southwestern cuisine that I was carrying around in my head. There was a gap to be filled and I was ready to fill it.

What was my image of contemporary southwestern cuisine to be carried out in Café Terra Cotta? First, it would be based on the fundamental ingredients native to the American Southwest and northern Mexico — chiles, corn, tomatoes, squash, and beans. Second, it would reach deeper into Mexico, especially to the Yucatán, central Mexico, and Oaxaca, where the sauces are more robust, complex, and balanced. Third, it would combine classical French and contemporary cooking techniques and presentation styles with an emphasis on absolutely fresh ingredients.

In the way it combines these three qualities, my image of contemporary southwestern cuisine is less Mexican than what you would find in New Mexico. My image is influenced more by the California cuisine that emerged in the 1970s and 1980s. Also, it is not so directly influenced by Native American cuisine, except to the degree that many of the most important foods (including corn and beans) were first cultivated by Native Americans.

Additionally, since Café Terra Cotta was by design a café, I did not want the food presentation to be viewed as an art form. Attractive presentation is certainly important, but I wanted the customers to be impressed by the taste of the food, not awed by its looks.

Given this overall concept, the one word that describes my food philosophy is *flavorful*. Flavorful doesn't necessarily mean spicy or hot. Flavorful includes the robust taste of our Black Bean Chili, the subtlety of our Garlic Custard, and the spiciness of our Jalapeño Ravioli. I have no desire to eat bland food. If I cannot recall the food flavors in a restaurant 24 hours after the meal, there is little chance that the restaurant will see me again. This places me in the category of people who live to eat rather than those who eat to live. My guess is that if you are reading this cookbook you are in the same category.

INGREDIENTS
THE BUILDING BLOCKS OF
SOUTHWESTERN CUISINE

A southwestern cookbook written ten years ago might have collected dust in most parts of the country for lack of the necessary ingredients. Now, fortunately, a variety of fresh and dried chiles, fresh cilantro, and tropical fruits like avocados, papayas, and mangoes are widely available across the country. More specialized produce such as jicama, chayote, and tomatillos have been around the Southwest for a long time, but are now making their way into mass distribution as well.

The following descriptions are not meant to be a comprehensive list of southwestern ingredients. (The section on chiles describes some eleven varieties out of more than 200 that exist.) Most of the fruits and vegetables used in southwestern cuisine are the familiar ones found in supermarkets across the country. I have concentrated on those ingredients that are used in the recipes in this book, plus a few which I hope will become more available and which would enhance many of these recipes.

ACHIOTE

Achiote is the dark red-brown seed of the annatto tree found in the tropics, used as a natural coloring in food and fabrics. It is a common ingredient in the Yucatán and southern Mexico that is being used more frequently in southwestern cuisine. It's used more for the orange-red color it gives to the food than for its barely discernible flavor, which is slightly acid. The rock-hard seeds must first be soaked in oil or water, then ground into a paste which is used to season chicken, pork, or fish. It is available from specialty Mexican product companies, either as whole seeds or already ground into a paste. We buy it in paste form, already ground and blended with black pepper, cumin, and oregano, which we thin as needed with orange juice. Both the seeds and the paste have a very long shelf life.

AVOCADOS

Avocados, a significant ingredient in southwestern cuisine, are now readily available throughout the year. Of the two major varieties, the darker, thick-skinned Hass and the green, thin-skinned Fuerte, I prefer the Hass. Avocados will ripen at room temperature, and are ready to eat when they give slightly to a gentle squeeze. They discolor quickly when exposed to air and should be used as soon as possible after they are cut. If you need to keep a cut avocado, sprinkle it with lemon or lime juice and cover it tightly with plastic wrap to minimize exposure to air.

BLACK BEANS

If I had a penny for every black bean served in Café Terra Cotta, I would....Well, I don't, so just let me rave about black beans. They are not native to the Southwest (they come from the Caribbean, and southern Mexico), but I think they make the best accompaniment to most southwestern entrees. They have more flavor than other beans, and their velvety color shines on the plate. When they are cooked to the proper consistency and seasoned right, I could make a complete meal of the Savory Black Beans on page 133.

CHAYOTE

This vegetable of the squash family, which looks like a light green Bartlett pear with large wrinkles, is becoming more and more available in grocery stores outside the Southwest and Deep South. The taste is somewhere between a cucumber and a zucchini squash. Chayotes need to be cooked and peeled. Thin slices add taste and texture to salads. The large central seed is

edible; remove it or cook it along with the rest of the fruit as you like.

CHEESES

Cheese is an essential ingredient in Mexican and southwestern cooking. In addition to adding flavor and texture, cheese has a cooling effect when combined with chiles. The butterfat in cheese is a better antidote to the blistering sting of a serrano or habanero chile than the glass of water that many people reach for (a little buttered bread has the same effect).

We use a variety of cheeses in our restaurants and in these recipes. Some are traditional, including Monterey jack and the fresh white Mexican-style *queso fresco*. We also use less traditional cheeses, such as Norwegian Jarlsberg, Italian fontina, Danish havarti, asiago, mozzarella, fresh goat cheeses such as Chevrion, Montrachet, or Laura Chenel's California Chèvre, and an occasional blue cheese. Any Swiss type can be substituted for Jarlsberg, and Parmesan for asiago. Monterey jack could take the place of fontina, although the flavor will not be the same. Follow your personal preferences.

CHILES

A discussion of southwestern cuisine without a discussion of chiles is impossible. Chiles are the foundation as well as the superstructure of southwestern cuisine. Chiles are found in many different cuisines, but nowhere else except in Mexico are they as significant. The more than 200 varieties of chiles could easily take up a whole book. I have limited my discussion to those varieties that we use a Café Terra Cotta and those that are readily available.

There are two ways of classifying chiles: first, by their level of heat, and second, whether they are fresh or dry. The degree of heat can be generalized in each chile, but it is important to understand that within a single variety the level of heat can vary considerably. It can vary due to the time of year or the weather, and even from one chile to the next on a single plant. With rare exceptions one cannot assume the level of heat

in an individual chile. I have heard of one sure-fire test: cut the chile in half and inhale deeply — if you don't go blind it's mild. This may be true, but I don't recommend it.

The number of chiles next to the descriptions below indicate the general level of heat. One chile is mild, but still hotter than a bell pepper. Four chiles is very serious heat.

You can exercise some control over the heat of chiles by using or removing the seeds and ribs, where the heat is most concentrated. Some recipes specify when the seeds and ribs are to be removed; otherwise, they are meant to be included. Of course, follow your own tastes and judgment.

For additional reading on chiles, I recommend the Mexican cookbooks by Rick Bayless, Diana Kennedy, and Patricia Quintana (see bibliography, page 158). An especially good source book is Mark Miller's *Great Chile Book*.

FRESH CHILES

When shopping for fresh chiles, choose those that are shiny and firm rather than blemished or shriveled. For ease in roasting, try to choose the ones with the fewest deep creases or bends. Fresh chiles keep best in the refrigerator, either loose in the vegetable bin or in a paper bag (plastic bags retain moisture, and chiles stored in plastic tend to deteriorate faster). If bought in good shape and refrigerated properly, fresh chiles should keep 5 to 10 days.

Anaheim: Anaheims are one of the most common chiles and are available in almost every supermarket coast to coast. They are very mild, but they are acceptable for "starter" dishes and salsas. Anaheims are usually bright green, 4 to 6 inches long. They should be peeled and take on an improved flavor when roasted. As with most chile peppers, there is more heat near the stem and in the veins. We rarely use Anaheims at Café Terra Cotta. When the red stage is available, however, they make a colorful addition to the plate.

Other long green chiles, similar in size and shape to Anaheims, can be substituted. Some

15

varieties, especially those grown in New Mexico, can be hotter than a typical Anaheim chile.

ᐖᐖ *Poblano:* Poblanos are my favorite chile. It is hard to believe, but when we opened Café Terra Cotta, poblanos were not available in Tucson, even though they passed through here on their way from Mexico to California. Now they are readily available in Tucson and in many other cities. Poblanos are dark green, wider at the stem end than Anaheims, and only 3-4 inches long. Although they are usually medium-hot, they can be surprisingly mild or fiery hot. When we have *chiles rellenos* (stuffed chiles) on the menu we prefer using poblanos and it is possible to find a very hot one and a mild one on the same plate. Poblanos are almost always roasted, except when we use them raw in salsas. This chile is often sold in supermarkets under the incorrect name *pasilla*, especially in California.

ᐖᐖᐖ *Jalapeño:* Jalapeños are the most readily available hot chiles. They are probably available in 99 percent of grocery stores today. They vary in length from 1½ to 3 inches. They are available fresh year round and are called for in many of the recipes in this book. If you want to reduce the heat of one of my recipes containing jalapeños, I recommend reducing the amount of jalapeños rather than substituting a milder chile.

For a drink with an extra kick, try cutting two or three jalapeños lengthwise, leaving the seed pod intact, and stuff them down the neck of a bottle of vodka or tequila. After two weeks use the vodka for Bloody Marys or, with tequila, Bloody Marias.

ᐖᐖᐖ *Serrano:* We don't use these small green chiles as often as I would like. They are about the same length as the jalapeño, but thinner and, therefore, more time-consuming to work with in a high-volume restaurant. This is less of a problem for the home cook who will be handling just a few chiles at a time, so feel free to use serranos whenever jalapeños are called for. Even though they are smaller than jalapeños, start by substituting them one for one; a serrano packs about the same amount of heat as a jalapeño in a smaller size. The flavor is also a

bit different, with more of a crisp sting compared to the more mellow heat of a jalapeño. A salsa fresca with finely chopped serranos is guaranteed to spice up your life.

ᐖᐖᐖᐖ *Habanero:* Hottest of the hot! Small and shaped like a bell pepper or pimiento, the habanero is the hottest chile on the market. If you find some, and you really like chiles, give them a try. Handle very carefully and use very sparingly. There is also a dried version, which can be crumbled and used like *chiltepín* or wherever dried chile flakes are used.

DRIED CHILES

Dried chiles are a key ingredient in southwestern cuisine. They are increasingly available in better grocery stores and through specialty mail-order firms. If you travel to Mexico, you can bring them back into the States; just remember to declare them at the agricultural inspection point. Hispanic markets in major cities, especially in the southwest, are another possibility. The point is that dried chiles have a very long shelf life if properly stored, so it pays to buy them in quantity when you have an opportunity.

When buying chiles by mail, choose a reputable company (see page 157). When selecting them in the market, look, feel, and smell. The chiles should be unbroken, with no white spots (which could indicate insects or mold). They should feel somewhat soft (if too hard and brittle, they are from an older crop), and the aroma should be rich and spicy. Store dried chiles in an airtight container in a cool, dark place. If the chiles are not used for an extended period of time, check them occasionally and discard any bad ones.

Dried chiles generally need to be rehydrated before using (see page 25). Pre-ground chile powder is a barely acceptable second choice for whole chiles; in the few recipes where it is called for, buy powder with a good strong color and use it promptly. If you have good dried chiles on hand, you can grind them to a powder yourself in an electric coffee or spice grinder.

❧ *California/New Mexico:* These are the ripened and dried version of the Anaheim chile and its New Mexico relatives. They are often sold in the Mexican section of supermarkets as "dried chili pods." Like their fresh counterparts, California chiles tend to be a little milder than New Mexico.

❧❧ *Ancho:* Ancho chiles are dried poblanos. However, you will find people calling fresh poblanos anchos and anchos (in the true dried form) pasillas or mulatos. Anchos are somewhat sweet and are used extensively in sauces and in moles. Anchos are available in specialty stores. You may find them in the spice section of grocery stores packaged in cellophane.

❧❧ *Cascabel:* Cascabel chiles are dark red and globe shaped, with a nutty flavor. When intact, the seeds make a rattling sound when the pod is shaken. Cascabels are harder to find in supermarkets, but may be found in Mexican grocery stores. Try them as a substitute for other chiles in sauces like the one on the Southwestern Meat Loaf on page 120, or in place of the chipotles in Lamb Chops with Dried Cherry-Chipotle Sauce (page 124).

❧❧ *Mulato:* Mulatos look like anchos in size and shape. They are slightly larger and darker, with a deeper, richer flavor. Mulatos are an essential ingredient in authentic Mexican moles, but they are not as widely available here, so I just call for anchos in the recipes.

❧❧ *Pasilla:* Pasilla chiles are long (5-7 inches), slender, dark brown, and somewhat wrinkled. They are moderately hot and are used in sauces and mole. They are often labeled *chile negro* in stores. If pasillas are not available, anchos can be substituted.

❧❧❧ *Chipotle:* Chipotles are fully ripe jalapeños that have been dried and smoked over embers. They are available in dried form as well as canned in vinegar-based *adobo;* the latter is more convenient, as dried chipotles are hard to rehydrate. Chipotles are quite hot and have an interesting smoky quality to them. We use them extensively in sauces at Café Terra Cotta.

❧❧❧ *Tepín:* Variously spelled chile tepín and chiltepín, these tiny dried chiles make up for their small size by their fiery heat. When fresh they are green to red (although I've never seen them sold fresh in this country), and they turn reddish brown when dried. Use sparingly. Chile pequín, another tiny dried chile, can be used as a substitute. Where they are crumbled into a dish, you can substitute other small dried chiles, including chile japonés, serrano seco, or chile de arbol. The red pepper flakes sold in spice racks should be a last resort.

CILANTRO

Next to chiles, this herb is *the* defining ingredient in southwestern cuisine. We don't use it in any of our desserts, but you are as likely as not to find it in everything else, either as an ingredient or as a garnish. Also known as Chinese parsley or fresh coriander, cilantro is now readily available throughout the country. Its appearance is very similar to Italian parsley, but its taste is distinct. Some people believe cilantro has a "soapy" taste. I don't, but I do agree that it is an acquired taste. An important characteristic of cilantro is that the finer you chop it, the less taste it has; chopped too fine it adds nothing but green coloring to the dish. At Café Terra Cotta, we always chop cilantro coarsely and at the last minute.

CUMIN

Cumin is a very important spice in both southwestern and Mexican cuisine. It is an ingredient in store-bought chili powder. I do not recommend buying cumin powder; to obtain the best cumin flavor and impact, buy whole cumin seeds and toast and grind them as needed. Cumin seeds can also be used whole in certain dishes.

EPAZOTE

Epazote is an herb that is very common in southern Mexico, particularly Oaxaca. It is also known as "pig weed," perhaps because its odor is not very pleasant and somewhat reminiscent of creosote. However, the flavor epazote imparts to a dish is very different from its odor. Epazote is not easy to find in this country. If you find it and like it, I would recommend you find a nursery that sells epazote plants and plant it. Remember, however, it is a weed and grows like one. Be sure to try a sprinkling of epazote in black beans. It has a positive effect on flavor and reduces the anti-social effect of beans.

GREEN ONIONS

Several recipes call for green onions or scallions. They may be used as a substitute for yellow or white onions in most salsas, or grilled whole as a garnish. Remember the green stem part is just as tasty as the white part.

HOJA SANTA

Hoja santa, literally "holy leaf," is common in southern Mexico, but next to impossible to find in this country. Its slight anise-sassafras-mint flavor is used in Oaxaca's famous yellow mole and in many of its stews. Hoja santa is a large shrub-like tree with leaves similar in shape to fig leaves, but with a softer texture. It should be used fresh since it does not dry very well. Because it is almost impossible to find here, I have not called for it in any of the recipes, but if you find some, try it with black beans, or in a simple quesadilla, or in the Tortilla Soup on page 73. It's also a nice addition to the mole verde for quail on page 115.

JICAMA

Jicama is a root vegetable of Mexican origin that is easy to describe, but if you haven't tasted it, difficult to imagine. It is shaped somewhat like a turnip. Its skin is light brown, thin, but tough and must be peeled. The inside flesh of jicama is white, with the texture of a radish, but not the bite. Traditionally it is served raw. However, sliced ¼ inch thick and grilled, it takes on a whole different flavor, sweet rather than starchy. We often use a saguaro-shaped cookie cutter to cut out miniature cactus shapes, grill them, and use them as a garnish on salads or main dishes.

MANGOES

Mangoes are one of my favorite fruits, ranking just behind papayas. If the large seed were as easy to remove as those of a papaya, they might jump ahead. Although the flavor is different, mangoes can be used interchangeably with papayas in the salad and salsa recipes in this book. When choosing ripe mangoes, look for a slight softness in the skin and a sweet, ripe, fruity smell. The less green color in the skin, the riper the mango; the fully ripe color may be red or yellow depending on the variety.

MUSHROOMS

With the exception of the Mushroom, Jarlsberg, and Parsley Salad on page 94, we do not use the common "button" mushroom. I prefer the more exotic varieties which, thanks to the exploding popularity of mushrooms, are no longer really exotic. Shiitake, oyster, and portabella mushrooms are finding their way into my recipes with increasing frequency. I think over the next few years we will see an even greater variety of fresh mushrooms hit the market.

Remember that mushrooms tend to act like a sponge and absorb water. Many mushrooms can simply be brushed clean, but if you do need to wash them, minimize the time mushrooms and water are in contact with each other.

NOPALES

Nopales are the fresh pads of prickly pear cactus. They are available in Mexican grocery stores and in many supermarkets in the Southwest. As the influence of Mexican and southwestern cuisine grows, you can expect to see them more readily available in other parts of the country. They are generally seasonal, since you really want to use only young new pads, which appear in spring and fall. When using fresh nopales, make sure all of the stickers are removed. Nopales can be grilled to add flavor and diced to use in salads or salsas. You can also find canned nopales, but they do not compare to fresh. If you can find fresh nopales, try them in salsas in place of apples, pears, and other crisp fruits.

NUTS AND SEEDS

Nuts and seeds, including hazelnuts, walnuts, pecans, pumpkin seeds, and pine nuts, play important roles in many recipes in this book. The same rules for purchase and storage apply to all of them. First, make sure they are fresh; because of their high oil content they can go rancid quickly. If buying them in bulk, taste them for freshness. Store them in a tightly sealed container and use them promptly.

Toasting brings out the flavor in all nuts and seeds, especially pine nuts. Larger nuts can be toasted on a sheet pan in a 350°F oven. Smaller seeds like pine nuts or sesame seeds are easier to handle in a skillet on top of the stove.

OIL

Unless a particular oil is called for in a recipe, "oil" means a vegetable oil with a high smoke point, such as peanut oil. This is the best kind to use for sauteing and deep-frying, when other oils might burn and impart a bitter taste to the food. More flavorful oils with lower smoke points, such as olive and walnut, are used mostly for flavoring rather than cooking.

PAPAYAS

Papayas are one of my favorite fruits. They have many uses in salsas, sauces, soups, and desserts. Their texture can be used to offset apples or pears in salsas; their sweetness can be used to balance the bite of chiles. Papayas are generally available all year thanks in part to our neighbors in Mexico. We do have periods, however, when they are scarce or expensive and are not the quality needed for restaurant use. If you are in Mexico, the Caribbean, or Hawaii and you have a chance to see how they are grown, take advantage of the opportunity. A papaya tree is a little different. The papayas are clustered at the top of the trunk, not out on branches.

To choose a fresh papaya, follow the same rules as for mangoes (see page 19), although the fully ripe skin color is yellow to orange, never red. If the papayas you find are unusually good, try cutting them in half, remove all the little black seeds, and serve as you would a half melon with a lime wedge.

STOCKS

Stocks are the basis for many classical sauces as well as soups. At Café Terra Cotta, we use a light chicken stock for most of our soups and some entree sauces. A few entrees in this book call for a reduced brown stock made from beef or veal bones, but the basic chicken stock in more reduced form can perform this role as well.

Two hours of simmering is enough time to extract the best flavors from poultry bones; any longer tends to break down the bones and can cause the stock to be bitter or cloudy. Meat stocks, on the other hand, require anywhere from 6 to 12 hours to achieve full flavor, and can be simmered all day or overnight. Never add salt to a stock until its final use, otherwise you could end up concentrating the salt as the stock reduces.

BASIC CHICKEN STOCK
Makes 4 quarts

    5 pounds chicken bones
    4 onions, halved (use skins too, if clean)
    4 carrots, washed
    2 ribs celery, washed
    1 bunch parsley, washed
    2 tomatoes, washed
    4 bay leaves
    12 peppercorns

Put all the ingredients in a large pot and add water to cover. Bring to a boil, skimming off the foam that comes to the surface. Reduce the heat and simmer, skimming occasionally, for 2 hours. Strain and discard the bones and vegetables.

BROWN VEAL STOCK

Replace the chicken bones in the previous recipe with veal, beef, or lamb bones. Place the bones and 2 of the onions in a roasting pan and roast in a 500°F oven for 1 hour. Transfer to the stockpot with the remaining ingredients, add water, and proceed as above, simmering the stock for 6 to 12 hours.

TOMATILLOS

Most people assume that the tomatillo is related to the tomato. Not so. It is part of the gooseberry family. A tomatillo looks very much like a small green tomato, but with an inedible parchment-like husk. When you peel the husk back and take it off the surface is very sticky and must be washed. A tomatillo with the husk peeled back and left on, however, makes an attractive garnish. We use raw tomatillos frequently in salsas for their tart flavor, and less frequently in cooked sauces. Cooked, they are less attractive, and cooking them brings out a sour flavor which needs to be balanced with stock and seasonings, as in the mole verde for quail on page 115.

TOMATOES

Ripe, home-grown tomatoes will always be my standard for tomato flavor, but they are not always available. The oval Roma tomatoes are usually the best to be found in supermarkets; they have fewer seeds, giving more useful yield, and they tend to have a little sweeter taste than others. Shop around, find the best that are available, and consider other fruits for salsa when good tomatoes are not to be found.

To peel and seed tomatoes, first cut out the core, then drop them into boiling water for 10 seconds and remove with a slotted spoon. The skin will slip off easily. Cut the peeled tomatoes in half horizontally, and gently squeeze each half to pop out the seeds.

COOKING EQUIPMENT
AND TECHNIQUES

There are very few specialized cooking utensils or techniques required to complete the recipes in this book. The recipes have been written assuming that the reader has a standard kitchen and a basic set of cookware. I also assume you have good sharp knives and know how to use them to slice, dice, and mince, and that you know how to roast a chicken and broil a steak, and what saute means. Following are some general thoughts on cookware and information on a few specialized cooking techniques that are characteristic of southwestern cooking and appear several times in the recipes.

Good pots and pans are essential. I prefer heavy gauge aluminum, either clad with stainless steel or anodized, for its heat-conducting properties. Copper conducts heat even better, but copper cookware is heavy and expensive, and requires too much maintenance to be practical for most kitchens. Aluminum cookware is somewhat controversial; although the connection has not been proven beyond a reasonable doubt, some people are concerned about health problems from aluminum absorbed into the food. A heavy core of aluminum with an outer surface of stainless steel or an anodized coating provides the best combination of heat efficiency, easy care, and affordability. Copper-core stainless pans such as those made by All-Clad are another good choice, but more expensive.

Good whisks are also important for mixing sauces, dressings, and many pastry preparations. Whisks come in various sizes, weights, and shapes, and there is a logical reason for choosing the right one for a given task. A whisk for sauces should be flexible, while one used for mixing heavy ingredients like cake batters should be stiffer. The whisk also needs to fit the bowl or saucepan; a whisk with wires 2 inches longer than the depth of the bowl or the width of the saucepan is just right, as it won't fall in when left unattended or become too hot and burn your hand.

The only specialized equipment needed for the recipes in this book are a blender or food processor for pureeing, a spice grinder (which can be a coffee grinder dedicated to this use), a pasta machine for the jalapeño ravioli (I recommend the hand-cranked version), a wok with a lid and a round cake rack for stove-top smoking (see page 23), and if possible, an outdoor grill.

STOVE-TOP SMOKING

Anyone who frequents restaurants will have noticed how popular smoked foods have become, and not just in southwestern cuisine. The smoky flavor of foods cooked over smoldering mesquite wood probably evokes a very southwestern image of cowboys sitting around an open fire. But I believe it's more than that: smoking is part of an overall trend to more flavorful food that goes far beyond cowboy country. The same adventurous palates that are drawn to Mexican chiles, Thai spices, and Mediterranean herbs also tend to appreciate the stronger flavors and subtle nuances of smoked foods.

Smoking foods used to be reserved for large-scale commercial establishments like fish smokehouses or do-it-yourself backyard smokers. Smaller commercial units have become popular with restaurants, but they are still not really practical for the home cook. It wasn't until a trip to Pau in southwestern France that I was introduced to smoking foods on top of the stove. While visiting the kitchen of André Daguin's Hôtel de France I discovered a metal box much like a *pain de mie* pan that he used for smoking such things as duck confit over oak sawdust. He told me the box was available in Brussels, if I might be passing that way. I didn't have Brussels on my itinerary that trip, but I realized that Chinese cooks do the same thing in a wok with rice and tea as the smoking fuel. I figured I would try wood chips in a wok, and it worked fine.

A basic stovetop smoking setup consists of a wok, a lid, a round wire cake rack that fits inside the wok, and wood chips (any type of wood except pine; we use mesquite). Smoking ruins the finish for stir-frying, but woks are cheap, so it makes sense to devote one just to smoking. Soak the wood chips in water at least a half hour, drain, and place in the bottom of the wok. Put the wire rack over the wet chips. Put the food to be smoked on the rack, cover the wok, and set over medium heat. Within a few minutes, the wood chips will begin to smolder, providing the aromatic smoke as the food roasts in the covered pan.

At Café Terra Cotta, we smoke not only meats, but poultry, fish, and vegetables. The smoking step is often combined with other cooking methods. While some foods can cook all the way in the smoker, like the pork tenderloins on page 128, others start out with a period of time in the smoker and finish in the oven or on the grill.

ROASTING AND PEELING CHILES

Large chiles and bell peppers have a waxy outer skin that is hard to digest, and shrivels in an unattractive way when the peppers are cooked. There are numerous ways to go about peeling chiles, but the one favored by most southwestern cooks is roasting, which also adds flavor.

Some roasting and peeling techniques are better suited for home use and some for restaurant or quantity preparation. The easiest home method I've used is to place the whole chiles directly on the burner, gas or electric, using high heat. Rotate them every minute or two until the skin is thoroughly charred. Put the charred chiles into a paper or plastic bag and let them sweat about 10 minutes, then slide the skin off under running water. Remove the stems and seeds by cutting a slit in the side and rinsing under water. Putting the chiles directly on the electric burner surprisingly does not make a mess; but if you prefer, there is a type of grate called an *asador* sold in cookware stores that keeps the chiles off the surface but close enough to the heat to char. Another home method is to broil the chiles until the skin is charred. I personally think this method takes too long and therefore cooks the flesh of the chiles more than I like.

There are two methods that can be used to roast large quantities of peppers. What we do at Café Terra Cotta is lay all the chiles out on a hot grill to char, and then dunk them into a cold sink or large bowl of cold water for 10 minutes to loosen the skins. You can do the same thing on a smaller scale on a home barbecue. The second quantity method is to deep-fry the chiles in a commercial fryer for 20 to 30 seconds, then dunk them into the cold water bath as above. The only disadvantage to this method is there is no charred flavor.

REHYDRATING DRIED CHILES

Unless dried chiles are to be ground to a powder or cooked in enough liquid that they rehydrate in the cooking process, they need to be soaked before being added to recipes. Place the chiles in a bowl and add boiling water to cover, and let steep until the chiles are soft. How long this takes depends on the variety; a thin-skinned California or New Mexico chile may take only a half hour, while a thick, dry chipotle can take up to 3 hours.

QUICK-SOAK PROCESS FOR BEANS

Cooking dried beans can sometimes take as much as 3 hours, but the time can be reduced by soaking the beans first. Anywhere from 6 hours to overnight is a typical soaking time, but you can't always plan that far ahead. A quicker soak in hot water can save an hour or so compared to starting from scratch. Place the washed beans in a large pot with water covering them by 3 to 4 inches. Bring them to a boil over medium heat. Remove the pan from the heat, cover, and let stand for 1 hour. Drain the beans and add water again to cover them by about 2 inches. Bring to a boil and simmer until tender, about 1 hour. I prefer to add the salt about 15 minutes before the beans are done because I feel the salt has time to flavor the beans without making them tough. Adding epazote (see page 18) when cooking the beans is supposed to remove the gaseous qualities from them.

GRILLING

When a non-southwesterner thinks of southwestern cuisine, the first mental picture conjured up is probably what I call "cowboy cuisine" — cowhands sitting around a campfire eating steaks and beans and drinking coffee with floating grounds that stick in their teeth. (To be honest, when we were in the catering business we helped fulfill some of these images.)

As I've said before, contemporary southwestern cuisine is not cowboy cuisine. Nevertheless, the slightly smoky flavor of foods cooked over an open fire is one of the basic elements of southwestern cuisine. Grilling, particularly over the mesquite wood which is native to the Southwest, has become a symbol of the Southwest, and has spread with the popularity of southwestern cuisine. I've had mesquite grilled food (real mesquite wood or mesquite charcoal) in New York City, Florida, Cleveland, and even the Outer Banks of North Carolina.

At Café Terra Cotta we grill a lot of our foods, but over a gas flame, not mesquite. Grilling over an open flame not only cooks faster (a real issue in a restaurant), but it imparts a flavor. Some of it comes from the fuel, especially from a wood fire, less so from charcoal; but a surprising amount of the flavor of grilled foods comes from the smoke caused by dripping fat or other juices, regardless of the heat source.

Mesquite wood gives off a very distinct flavor and one that can be very strong. It also burns very hot and throws a lot of sparks and ash. We do not use it for all these reasons, but mainly because the flavors of our food come from the sauces, marinades, and accompaniments. We do use mesquite chips in the smoker, where the smoky flavor is easier to control.

For the home cook with a typical backyard grill, I suggest a combination of ordinary charcoal briquets for fuel and wood chips for flavor. In my experience, briquets provide more control over the heat of the fire than charcoals made from specific woods such as hickory and mesquite. The amount of smoky flavor is also easy to vary with the heat of the fire and the amount of wood chips you use. It is important to soak the wood chips before using; otherwise they will burn too quickly and emit little or no smoke. Experiment with the amount of wood chips you like, and remember that a slower fire allows more time for the smoke flavor to permeate the food.

The only place we do cook with wood is in our wood-fired pizza oven. Pecan wood is plentiful in southern Arizona because of the large pecan orchards in this area. Pecan burns with a steady heat and imparts a very mild flavor. When our customers swear they taste the wood flavor in the pizzas, I just smile. I think it's mostly in their imagination and comes from the overall smell of the restaurant when they first come in the front door.

I am concerned about the talk of carcinogens in grilled foods, but address these concerns by heavy trimming of fat from meat and by not over-grilling and cremating the dish. As I understand it, the problem is mainly in foods that are burned on the surface, or from an excess of fat dripping on the fire and burning. Frankly, my concern is more a matter of taste than a fear of carcinogens; I don't like the excessively charred or downright burnt flavor that a too-hot fire or flaming drippings can give the food. A grill that can adjust the distance of the food from the fire is also helpful in this regard.

NOTES TO THE COOK
MISCELLANEOUS INGREDIENTS AND MEASUREMENTS

Keep in mind that every cook has a personal idea of what is meant by "oil," "butter," "pinch," "dash," even "eggs" when reading and producing a recipe. That's the reason it is very difficult to replicate precisely a dish you ate at a friend's house or at your favorite restaurant. It comes down to constantly tasting and adjusting in order to reach the final result.

◆ I have tried to be specific when necessary when calling for **oil.** If not, use a mild vegetable oil such as corn or peanut. As for **butter,** I always mean unsalted butter, because it gives you control over the final seasoning. I feel salted butter has absolutely no place in baking especially when sweetness is involved.

◆ **Cream** in the recipes means heavy or whipping cream without any additives, sometimes called manufacturing cream. In some areas all the cream you can find in supermarkets is ultra-pasteurized, which is acceptable, but if you have a choice, use the "natural" version.

◆ **Eggs** pose a problem in recipes at times, particularly cakes and some other desserts. I prefer to use extra large eggs, although large eggs are acceptable for the recipes in this book.

◆ **Measurements** also vary from person to person. My pinch will certainly be different from that of someone six foot two with huge hands. Again, just taste.

◆ There is a difference between **dry and wet measuring cups.** The difference can be a couple of tablespoons. Usually wet measuring cups have a spout and are glass or plastic. Most often dry measuring cups are metal. There can also be a difference in dry measuring depending, for instance, on whether you scoop flour up with the cup or spoon the ingredient into the cup. I prefer to use the spooning method myself. It gives a lighter result.

◆ The final measurement rule, as I have said before, comes down to **taste.** All along the way you must taste. That is why you find many cooks who never eat their own meals. By the time dinner is ready, they have tasted everything and are full enough without indulging in a meal.

MENU PLANNING

When choosing recipes from this book for a meal, please keep in mind what I call balance. Try not to repeat major ingredients, such as pairing an appetizer and an entree that both use cheese. Unless you are bent on destruction (or just love hot flavors) don't use recipes with chiles in every course. Balance also means to take into account the colors you will present on your plate. Green and brown may taste all right together but a touch of red somewhere might make all the difference in eye appeal.

Try the following menu combinations:

EGGPLANT, PROSCIUTTO, AND FONTINA (PAGE 57)
PORK TENDERLOIN WITH APRICOT CHUTNEY
(PAGE 128)
SAVORY BLACK BEANS (PAGE 133)
CRÈME BRULÉE (PAGE 144)

GARLIC CUSTARD (PAGE 46)
QUAIL IN ESCABECHE WITH MOLE VERDE
(PAGE 115)
AUTUMN TULIPE WITH SPICED APPLE ICE CREAM (PAGE 138)

WARM GOAT CHEESE WITH RED PEPPER SAUCE
(PAGE 56)
LAMB CHOPS WITH TEQUILA AND HONEY
(PAGE 126)
ARIZONA PRINCESS CAKE (PAGE 137)
OR
DIVINE MADNESS (PAGE 145)

TORTILLA "LASAGNA" (PAGE 54)
BLACK BEAN AND SMOKED CORN SALSA
(PAGE 41), WARMED AS A SIDE DISH
CHOCOLATE MOUSSE PIE (PAGE 151)

WINES
WITH SOUTHWESTERN CUISINE

Both my husband, who is responsible for our wine lists, and I believe in the marriage of food and wine. Although many people think of beer and margaritas when they are ordering southwestern food, we almost always think wine. Usually red wine, but almost always wine.

In selecting or pairing wine with southwestern food, or for that matter, with any cuisine, there is really only one rule. That is, ignore rules and drink what you like! That means taking anyone else's opinions, even mine, with a large grain of salt (or 6 ounces of Cabernet). If you find your preferences close to mine, fine. If they are vastly different or opposite, that's fine too. The key is your taste buds, not self-proclaimed experts.

This discussion on wine concentrates totally on California wines. We don't mean to ignore the fine wines from other states and countries, but given our cuisine we made the conscious decision to concentrate on California wines.

Wine is an acquired taste and one that changes over time. Most often people start with a white or blush (pink) wine, generally one that is reasonably priced and not terribly complex. As one develops a taste for wine, one usually find a preference for either red or white. Blush wines, usually White Zinfandel, generally do not stand up to southwestern cuisine, and in my opinion are not really "food" wines.

Another point that needs to be made before discussing individual varietals and wineries is the issue of "white wines with fish and poultry, red wines with meat." Feel free to ignore this rule if you are so inclined. I do and have never been embarrassed by a waiter or sommelier questioning my choice. David Rosengarten and Joshua Wesson have a book on this subject called *Red Wine with Fish* (Simon and Schuster, 1989).

The route to white wines quite often starts and ends with Chardonnay. Ignoring the "jug" wines, Chardonnay outsells all other varietals, including Sauvignon Blanc, Chenin Blanc, Johannisberg Riesling, and Gewurztraminer. Many people, faced with wine lists that overwhelm all but seasoned wine drinkers, choose to not embarrass themselves and just order Chardonnay. Frankly, when pairing white wine with southwestern food, I put Chardonnay at the bottom of a list of the wines mentioned above. Consider instead a Sauvignon Blanc or Fumé Blanc. These two wines, both made from the Sauvignon Blanc grape, are often a better choice with our type of food than Chardonnay. They are as dry as or drier than most Chardonnays, with a grassy or herbaceous flavor that seems to pair nicely with assertive, spicy foods. I recommend the Sauvignon Blancs of Kenwood, Murphy-Goode, and Matanzas Creek, and Fumé Blancs by Robert Mondavi, Ferrari-Carano, and Chateau St. Jean's "Petite Etoile" Fumé.

If your preferences run to the sweeter wine and you are willing to admit it, try a Gewurztraminer. The sweetness of most Gewurztraminers, not to mention the distinctive spicy aroma, offers a foil to the spiciness of southwestern food. Fetzer's version is fairly priced, widely available, and an excellent choice, and it has been on our wine list since we opened. Other sweeter whites include Chenin Blanc and Johannisberg Riesling.

In recent years more and more wineries are blending two or more varietals. Some of these proprietary blends are more formally known as "meritage" wines (rhymes with "heritage"). Most meritage whites are Bordeaux-style blends of Sauvignon Blanc and Semillon, but some wineries take liberties and add non-Bordeaux varieties like Muscat to the blend. These wines are very individualistic, but in general tend to be more middle of the road between sweet and dry. My very favorite is a proprietary white blend from Caymus called "Conundrum." A close second is "Langtry Meritage White" by Guenoc. Both of these are excellent wines by top California wineries and go very well with our foods.

Other white varietals you might try with southwestern cuisine include Viognier, Marsanne, and Pinot Blanc. Some are just starting to come onto the market and are in very limited supply, but they are worth seeking out.

Cabernet Sauvignon is the best seller among red wine aficionados. However, when pairing with southwestern cuisine, I prefer a fruitier, less tannic wine. My first choice is a Syrah or Petite Syrah (sometimes spelled Sirah). These Rhône varietals have both a fruity and a spicy component that compliment spicy food; the spicy component echoes the spices in the food, while the fruity component offers a mellowing balance. Even if you have shied away from red wines, I urge you to try a nice Petite Syrah with one of these recipes. Stag's Leap Vineyard makes a Petite Syrah that is very drinkable and stands up to the spiciest of foods.

My second choice, and a close second, is Zinfandel (red, please!). Zinfandels generally have lots of fruit flavor, but are less spicy than a Syrah. I would choose this when you want to balance rather than emphasize the spicy flavors in the food. There are many great Zinfandels coming out of California these days. The choice is large in California and is getting better around the country. Some of the best Zinfandels that have been on our wine list at Café Terra Cotta are Kenwood's "Jack London" Zinfandel and the Zinfandels from Ridge Vineyards, Ravenswood, and DeLoach. By the way, if you insist on White Zinfandel, DeLoach's is among the very best.

If your red wine taste runs to the lighter and more mellow reds, then I would suggest pairing these recipes with Merlot or Pinot Noir. These wines, which one might think would not stand up to spicy foods, actually go very well. Our favorite Merlots include Duckhorn, Cuvaison, Newton, and Shafer. We have had Wild Horse Pinot Noir on our wine list for several years and enjoy it with our food. We also like the Zaca Mesa "Reserve" Pinot. Robert Mondavi also makes a great "Reserve" Pinot.

If you are a Cabernet fan and want to stick to Cabernets, then I suggest seeking out those that are less tannic; a very tannic wine seems to accentuate hot flavors. Cabernets tend to lose tannin with age, but older Cabernets are harder to find and can be significantly more expensive. Jordan Winery has a reputation for fine Cabernets that are very drinkable early. With other wineries that I can mention, it may be best to check with a knowledgeable wine person on the drinkability of a specific vintage from each winery. Popular Cabernets on our list come from Stag's Leap Wine Cellars, Caymus, Heitz, Joseph Phelps, and Silver Oak.

As with white wines, several less known varietals are beginning to emerge. Mataro or Mourvèdre, a Rhône varietal grown on a small scale in California, goes well with the recipes. So do several of the Bordeaux varietals other than Cabernet Sauvignon, including Cabernet Franc, Malbec, and Petit Verdot. You may find the latter varieties on their own as varietal wines, or blended with Cabernet Sauvignon and Merlot in red proprietary blends or "meritage" wines. Foremost of these are "Opus One," a joint project of Robert Mondavi and Chateau Mouton-Rothschild, "Langtry Meritage Red" by Guenoc, "Rubicon" by Neibaum Coppola, and "Cain 5" by Cain Cellars.

Again, I want to emphasize how important it is to trust your own taste buds. Wine salesmen, friends, and books can be good sources of information, but in the end, follow your own tastes. Drink what you like, in moderation with good food for the maximum enjoyment of both.

SALSAS

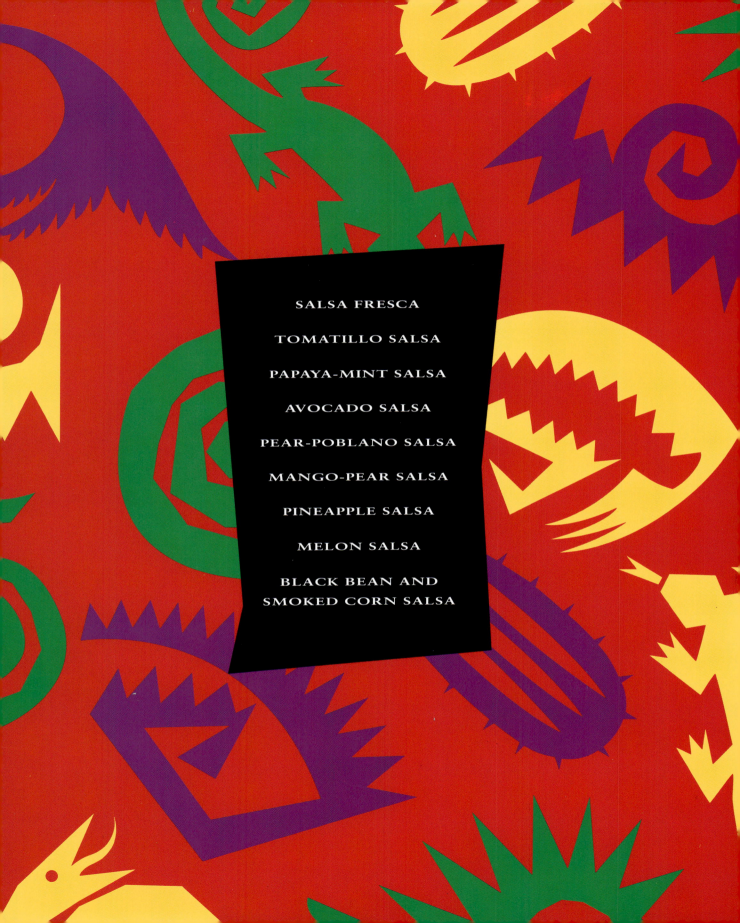

SALSA FRESCA

TOMATILLO SALSA

PAPAYA-MINT SALSA

AVOCADO SALSA

PEAR-POBLANO SALSA

MANGO-PEAR SALSA

PINEAPPLE SALSA

MELON SALSA

BLACK BEAN AND
SMOKED CORN SALSA

One cannot think of southwestern cuisine without thinking of salsa. Salsa, the Spanish word for sauce, can describe a variety of things; technically, a tomato-based sauce could be called a salsa. In contemporary southwestern cuisine, however, it has taken on a more narrow definition: a combination of chopped chiles, tomatoes or tomatillos, cilantro, and perhaps onions, used as a garnish, flavoring, or sauce for other foods. It can be fresh or cooked or come out of a jar. At Café Terra Cotta we prepare our salsas fresh every day, and in only one recipe (the stuffed shrimp on page 101) is the salsa cooked.

Traditional salsa recipes vary mainly in proportions and in variations in basic ingredients. One recipe might call for Anaheim chiles, another poblanos and another jalapeños. A recipe might suggest the green part of scallions while another might suggest the white. Another might leave out onions altogether.

More recently, salsas have seen no boundary, with other fruits and vegetables taking the place of tomatoes, and Café Terra Cotta is very much a part of that trend. Without going to extremes, we have served mango, cucumber, melon, and plum salsas, as well as such combinations as pineapple-pear, pineapple-papaya, apple-pear, and corn-avocado. Not every salsa goes with every dish, however, a lesson not necessarily learned in all restaurants. A very tart salsa might overpower a delicate fish, but could be just right with red meats or game.

Independent of the above combinations, I do encourage you to experiment. There are three basic and critical points in making a great salsa. First, the ingredients must be fresh. With a bounty of chiles available in almost every supermarket, there is no need for canned chiles. Second, the ingredients should be chopped by hand (no food processors), and they should be chopped to a uniform size. This is very important because if the ingredients are not of uniform size they will not mix well and you will not achieve the taste combination you are trying for. Third, the salsa should be served when it is fresh. Most fresh salsas have a short shelf life. I don't mind a head on my beer, but I do mind one on my salsa.

The quantities in the recipes here might seem large at first, but I think you will find these flavors addictive. Most are not terribly hot, so they are meant to be used liberally. We go through large quantities of all of them at the restaurant, and I suspect that once you make a batch you will find it disappears in no time.

SALSA FRESCA
(FRESH TOMATO SALSA)

〜〜〜〜〜

There are many, many versions of salsa fresca, probably as many versions as there are cooks. We serve salsa fresca with many of our fish and chicken dishes, and it's also delicious by itself with tortilla chips.

Makes 3 cups

1½ pounds tomatoes, cored, seeded, and cut into ½-inch dice

¼ cup finely chopped onion
¼ cup chopped cilantro
1 jalapeño or serrano chile, seeded, deveined, and finely chopped
3 tablespoons fresh lime juice
Salt and pepper, to taste

Mix all the ingredients together and let stand at least half an hour before serving. Use within 24 hours.

TOMATILLO SALSA

〜〜〜〜〜

Tangy green tomatillos and the colors from the other ingredients in this salsa add a vibrant splash of color to simple preparations of fish and chicken. This salsa really dresses up the salmon cakes on page 62. One jalapeño will be quite spicy so proceed with caution.

Makes 2 cups

8 tomatillos, husked, washed, and finely diced
1 small red bell pepper, seeded and finely diced
1 small yellow bell pepper, seeded and finely diced

1 small poblano chile, seeded and finely diced
1 jalapeño or serrano chile, finely chopped
2 tablespoons lime juice
Dash white wine vinegar
1 clove garlic, minced
Salt and pepper, to taste
Pinch of sugar

Combine all the ingredients, mix thoroughly, and set aside in the refrigerator for at least 2 hours for the flavors to combine. Use within 2 days.

PAPAYA-MINT SALSA

Not every salsa has to have chiles; sometimes a salsa's role is just to be moist, cool, and refreshing. This one is the perfect foil to spicy foods such as a quesadilla made with particularly hot chiles. It also works to cool down Scallops in Adobo (page 105).

Makes 3 cups

  1½ papayas, peeled, seeded, and cut into
     small chunks

½ red bell pepper, seeded and diced
3 tablespoons lime juice
1 tablespoon olive oil
2 tablespoons finely chopped mint
Salt and pepper, to taste

Combine all the ingredients, mix thoroughly, and set aside in the refrigerator for at least 2 hours for the flavors to combine. Use within 24 hours.

AVOCADO SALSA

I call this a salsa rather than guacamole because it is left chunky and uses less chile than I would for guacamole. It is a good garnish for many dishes such as grilled steak, the fish paillard on page 108, and the meat loaf on page 120, either in addition to the sauces given in those recipes or in their place.

Makes 3½ cups

  3 ripe avocados, pitted, peeled, and coarsely
     chopped
  2 ripe tomatoes, seeded and chopped

1 small red onion, chopped
½ jalapeño or 1 serrano chile, finely
    chopped
½ cup coarsely chopped cilantro
1 teaspoon minced garlic
¼ to ½ cup lime juice
Salt and pepper, to taste

Combine all the ingredients, mix thoroughly, and set aside in the refrigerator for at least 2 hours for the flavors to combine. Use within 24 hours.

MANGO-PEAR SALSA

This salsa goes nicely with spicy meat dishes. Fully ripe Bosc pears are the best choice for this salsa; they are not only sweet, they have a bouquet that others don't have. Papaya may be substituted for the mango.

Makes 3 cups

1 mango, peeled and diced
1 firm but ripe pear, cored and diced
½ yellow bell pepper, seeded and diced
½ red bell pepper, seeded and diced
½ poblano chile, seeded and diced
½ jalapeño or serrano chile, seeded and finely
   chopped
¼ cup chopped cilantro
2 tablespoons lime juice
1 teaspoon minced garlic
Salt and pepper, to taste

Combine all the ingredients, mix thoroughly, and set aside in the refrigerator for at least 2 hours for the flavors to combine. Use within 24 hours.

PEAR-POBLANO SALSA

Here again, the tastier the pear, the better your salsa. Try this in place of the mango salsa in Grilled Duck Breast with Mole Sauce (page 116).

Makes 4 cups

3 ripe but firm pears, cored and diced
½ poblano chile, seeded and diced
½ red bell pepper, seeded and diced
½ yellow bell pepper, seeded and diced
½ small red onion, diced
1 teaspoon minced garlic
¼ cup coarsely chopped cilantro
¼ cup lime juice, or to taste
Salt and pepper, to taste

Combine all the ingredients, mix thoroughly, and set aside in the refrigerator for at least 2 hours for the flavors to combine. Use within 24 hours.

PINEAPPLE SALSA

The sugar in this recipe takes the bite off the acidity of the pineapple. You can use less if you are lucky enough to find a truly ripe, sweet pineapple. Serve with fish.

Makes 3 cups

½ ripe pineapple cut into small chunks
    (about 2½ cups)
½ small red bell pepper, seeded and diced
1 jalapeño or serrano chile, seeded and finely
    chopped

½ cup coarsely chopped cilantro
¼ cup lime juice
⅛ cup olive oil
Salt and pepper, to taste

Combine all the ingredients, mix thoroughly, and set aside in the refrigerator for at least 2 hours for the flavors to combine. Use within 24 hours.

MELON SALSA

The contrast of the cool melon and spicy chile is the appeal of this salsa. Of course, season will dictate when you have the best melons available. This salsa is excellent with grilled swordfish or with the Three-Cheese Chiles Rellenos on page 48.

Makes about 3½ cups

½ small honeydew melon, cut into small
    chunks (about 1½ cups)
½ small cantaloupe, cut into small chunks
    (about 1½ cups)

1 jalapeño or serrano chile, finely chopped
¼ cup coarsely chopped cilantro
2 tablespoons lime juice
1 tablespoon olive oil
Salt and pepper, to taste

Combine all the ingredients, mix thoroughly, and set aside in the refrigerator for at least 2 hours for the flavors to combine. Use within 24 hours.

BLACK BEAN AND SMOKED CORN SALSA

During the last few years, the boundaries of salsa have expanded enormously, and I have to admit that this one is pushing the limits. In fact, I'm not sure whether to call it a salsa, a side dish, or a salad — it works in all three roles. Try it cold with grilled fish or chicken, or heated as a vegetable side dish to Shrimp Stuffed with Herbed Goat Cheese (page 101) or Grilled Shrimp with Achiote (page 104). For that matter, it could accompany almost any entree in this book. For a simpler version, omit the smoking step and use fresh or frozen corn kernels.

Makes 6 cups

6 ears of corn
½ pound black beans, cooked in salted
　　water with bay leaf, drained and cooled
1 medium red bell pepper, seeded and diced
1 teaspoon minced garlic
¼ red onion, chopped
1 jalapeño or serrano chile, finely chopped
¼ cup olive oil
Salt and pepper, to taste

Cook the corn in a stovetop smoker (see page 23) for 20 minutes. Let cool. Cut the kernels off the cobs, combine with the remaining ingredients, and mix thoroughly. Set aside in the refrigerator for at least 2 hours for the flavors to combine. Use within 3 days.

APPETIZERS

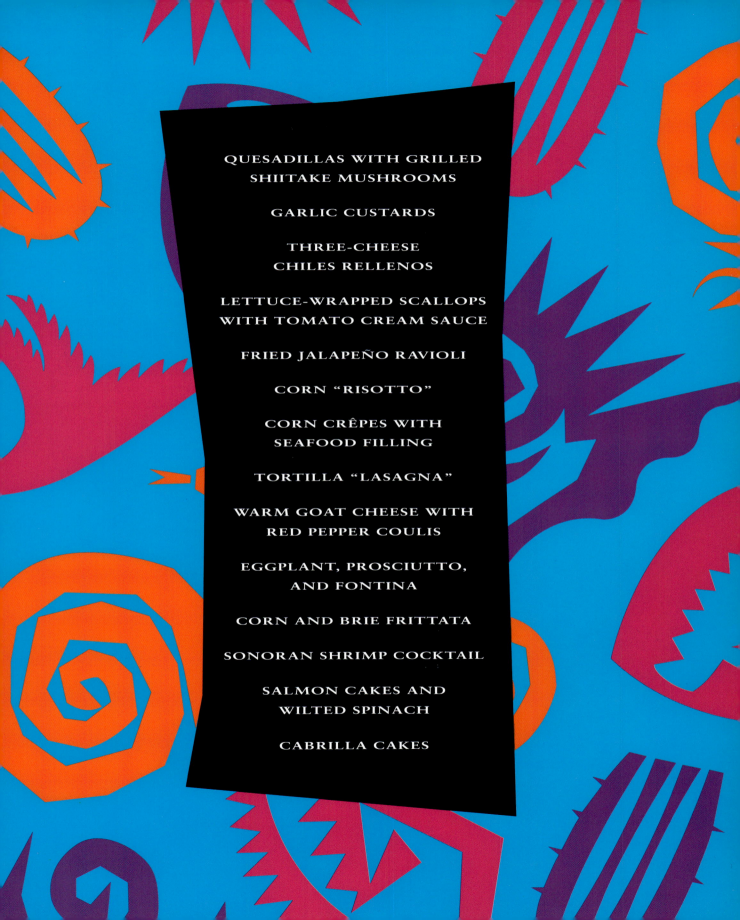

QUESADILLAS WITH GRILLED
SHIITAKE MUSHROOMS

GARLIC CUSTARDS

THREE-CHEESE
CHILES RELLENOS

LETTUCE-WRAPPED SCALLOPS
WITH TOMATO CREAM SAUCE

FRIED JALAPEÑO RAVIOLI

CORN "RISOTTO"

CORN CRÊPES WITH
SEAFOOD FILLING

TORTILLA "LASAGNA"

WARM GOAT CHEESE WITH
RED PEPPER COULIS

EGGPLANT, PROSCIUTTO,
AND FONTINA

CORN AND BRIE FRITTATA

SONORAN SHRIMP COCKTAIL

SALMON CAKES AND
WILTED SPINACH

CABRILLA CAKES

I have to admit that next to desserts, appetizers are my favorite category on a restaurant menu. I feel this way both as an executive chef and on those too few occasions when I am a customer at someone else's restaurant. For a chef, appetizers allow the most room for creativity, since restaurant customers generally are willing to be more adventuresome with appetizers than when ordering an entree. Entrees are usually the centerpiece of the meal and dishes that sound too innovative or have too many unusual ingredients may be passed over by all but true "foodies."

Appetizers, on the other hand, do not represent a major commitment and, therefore, allow for experimentation. At Café Terra Cotta, I allow our kitchen staff maximum creativity in developing new appetizers. We put these dishes on the menu under the heading of "Starters and Small Plates." This is the area on the menu where our first-time customers are most easily introduced to our cuisine. I have found that many of Terra Cotta's customers order the same way I do when I eat out, having several appetizers and a dessert. It provides a broader sampling of a restaurant's repertoire in a single visit and makes the meal a lot more fun.

The Starters and Small Plates section is also the part of the menu that has seen the most change, and prompted the most vocal reaction from customers. When their favorite item is replaced they have to be weaned from the old items to the new items and promised that their favorite will be back some day. There are two appetizers, however, that have been on Terra Cotta's menu from the day we opened and, in all likelihood, will always remain: Garlic Custard and Jalapeño Ravioli. Removing these might incite a riot. I've included recipes for these two all-time favorites along with many that have been popular at Café Terra Cotta.

Quesadillas
with Grilled Shiitake
Mushrooms and Jarlsberg

Quesadillas — cheese and other savory ingredients folded inside a tortilla and toasted on a griddle — are to Mexican cooking a little like what omelettes or crêpes are to French cuisine, that is, a catch-all for many flavors and flavor combinations. We have served many different versions at Café Terra Cotta; here is one of the favorites, in which shiitake mushrooms add their flavor and texture to commercial button or "garden variety" mushrooms. It could be made with button mushrooms alone if shiitakes are hard to come by or if you don't like their taste. Of course, the Jarlsberg cheese could be replaced with another cheese of your choice, and other wild and cultivated mushroom varieties such as chanterelles or portabella are also possible additions or substitutes.

Serves 8 (or 16 as an hors d'oeuvre)

¼ **pound fresh shiitake mushrooms**
2 **tablespoons oil**
Salt and pepper
¼ **pound button mushrooms**
½ **small onion, finely chopped**
8 **10-inch flour tortillas**
1½ **cups grated Jarlsberg cheese**
½ **cup Salsa Fresca (page 37)**

1. Remove and discard the shiitake stems and brush the tops with a small amount of the oil. Sprinkle with salt and pepper. Let stand for 10 minutes. Grill or broil until cooked through and limp; let cool, slice, and set aside.

2. Mince the button mushrooms and onion in the food processor or by hand. Heat the remaining oil in a skillet and cook the mushroom-onion mixture until the liquid evaporates. Season with salt and pepper to taste.

3. For each quesadilla, spread a little of the onion-mushroom mixture on one side of a tortilla. Sprinkle with sliced shiitakes and Jarlsberg, fold in half, and cook on a lightly greased griddle or nonstick skillet until browned, about 2 minutes per side. Cut each quesadilla into 4 wedges and serve with salsa fresca.

Variation: Quesadillas are a great way to use leftovers. Most anything can be turned into a quesadilla as long as there are enough moist ingredients to keep the overall quesadilla from turning out dry. You can also use just about any variety of cheese, except really hard ones like Parmesan. Try Italian Fontina with strips of roasted and peeled poblano chile and cooked mesquite-smoked bacon, or Monterey jack cheese with Black Bean and Smoked Corn Salsa (page 41).

GARLIC CUSTARDS

~~~~~~~~

This is a delightful savory custard that we serve as an appetizer or a "grazing" course. Although it stands on its own, it can be incorporated into a menu as a side dish. In place of the hazelnuts, try walnuts, pecans, or a mixture of nuts.

Serves 8

Custard
2 tablespoons roasted garlic (see page 111)
1 jalapeño chile, minced very fine
2 cups cream
4 egg yolks
2 whole eggs
¾ teaspoon salt
¼ teaspoon white pepper
⅛ teaspoon nutmeg

Vinaigrette
¼ cup red wine vinegar
¾ cup olive oil
1 teaspoon Dijon mustard
1 cup Salsa Fresca (page 37)

Herbed Hazelnuts
2 tablespoons butter
1 cup hazelnuts (filberts), toasted
¼ teaspoon each oregano and thyme, crumbled
Pinch of cayenne
⅛ teaspoon ground cumin, or to taste
Salt and pepper, to taste

1. Preheat the oven to 300°F. Butter 8 (4-ounce) ramekins. Blend the custard ingredients together thoroughly. Pour into the ramekins and place them in a baking pan. Place the pan in the oven and carefully add hot water to come halfway up the sides of the ramekins. Bake until a toothpick inserted in the center comes out clean, 45 to 50 minutes. Remove the pan from the oven and leave the custards in the water bath to keep warm for up to 20 minutes.

2. Whisk the vinaigrette ingredients together in a small saucepan and heat gently. Set aside to keep warm. Melt the butter in a skillet and saute the hazelnuts with their seasonings until the nuts are well coated. Chop coarsely.

3. To serve, turn the custards out of their ramekins onto plates. Spoon warm vinaigrette over each one and sprinkle with warm hazelnuts.

THREE-CHEESE CHILES RELLENOS

Americans normally think of a chile relleno as a chile stuffed with cheese, battered and deep-fried, and drenched in a chile sauce. In Mexico, chiles rellenos come in many forms. *Relleno* itself means stuffed but not necessarily battered or fried. This version is typical in that it is battered and fried, although the blue cheese filling is a little untraditional. Other cheeses may be substituted.

Chiles rellenos lend themselves to almost endless variation. These chiles can be served as an appetizer with your choice of salsa, or with the mole sauce for duck on page 116. The Red Chile Cream Sauce on page 121 is another possiblity. You can substitute either of the fillings for the Baked Stuffed Poblano Chiles in the entree chapter (see page 118) for this one and vice versa.

Serves 6 as an appetizer, 3 as an entree

6 Anaheim or poblano chiles

Filling
4 ounces goat cheese
2 ounces blue cheese
2 ounces cream cheese
2 cloves garlic, peeled and minced
2 tablespoons cilantro, minced
Salt and pepper, to taste

Beer Batter
6 eggs, separated
6 ounces beer
1½ cups all-purpose flour
½ teaspoon salt
⅛ teaspoon pepper

Oil for deep-frying
1½ cups Salsa Fresca (page 37) or Melon Salsa (page 40)

1. Roast and peel the chiles (see page 24). Make a slit in the side of each chile and remove the seeds, but not the stems. Set aside.

2. Combine the cheeses and blend with a wooden spoon or in an electric mixer. Add the garlic and cilantro and mix well. Season to taste with salt and pepper. Spoon the filling evenly into the chiles and set aside.

3. Combine the egg yolks and the remaining batter ingredients and beat with a whisk until stiff but smooth. In another bowl, beat the egg whites until stiff. Fold them into the batter.

4. Heat the oil to 375°F in a deep pan or in an electric fryer. Dip the filled chiles in the batter and fry until golden brown, 4 to 5 minutes.

LETTUCE-WRAPPED SEA SCALLOPS
WITH TOMATO CREAM SAUCE

As with many of the appetizers in this book, this dish can be served in larger portions as a main course with the addition of a side vegetable and/or starch.

Serves 6

    1 cup cream
    ½ cup peeled and seeded tomatoes, cut into
        medium dice
    Salt and pepper, to taste
    1 pound large sea scallops (16–20 count —
        see Note)
    10 to 12 large red lettuce leaves
    2 tablespoons chopped parsley

1. Preheat the oven to 450°F. Bring the cream to a boil in a skillet and reduce by half. Add the tomatoes and season with salt and pepper to taste. Keep warm.

2. Wrap the scallops individually in lettuce leaves, using half a large leaf per scallop. Arrange the packets seam side down in a baking dish and bake until the scallops are firm to the touch, about 5 minutes.

3. Transfer the scallops to warm plates and pour the sauce over the top. Garnish with chopped parsley.

Variation: Add ¼ cup chopped fresh basil to the sauce along with the tomatoes.

Note: When you buy scallops (or shrimp), the count per pound tells you the size; the higher the count, the smaller the scallop.

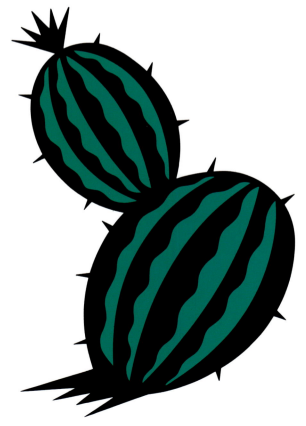

FRIED JALAPEÑO RAVIOLI

This was one of my original ideas when I set up the menu for Café Terra Cotta. I wondered whether fresh pasta could be deep-fried, and my experiences with fried sweet doughs told me to give it a try. At the same time, I had been experimenting with flavoring pasta with all sorts of things other than the standard tomato, beet juice, or spinach, and I figured, why not jalapeño chile? You can increase or decrease the amount of chile according to your own heat tolerance. The amount of flour needed for the pasta will vary according to the moisture created by the amount of pureed chiles.

Makes 24 (6 appetizer servings)

Filling
6 ounces ricotta cheese
4 ounces Monterey jack cheese, shredded
1 jalapeño chile, seeds and stem removed, minced
¼ cup cilantro
⅛ teaspoon ground cumin
⅛ teaspoon salt
Pinch of cayenne

Pasta
2 cups flour (approximately)
½ teaspoon salt
3 eggs
1 tablespoon olive oil
3 jalapeño chiles, seeds and stems removed

1 cup bread crumbs
¾ cup grated Parmesan cheese
3 eggs
Oil for deep-frying
Chopped cilantro, for garnish
¼ cup Salsa Fresca (page 37)

1. Combine all the filling ingredients in a bowl or a food processor. Taste for seasoning and adjust as needed.

2. To make the pasta by hand, place the flour and salt on a work surface. Make a well in the center. Beat the eggs and olive oil together. Puree the chiles in a processor (or mince them very finely) and add to the egg mixture. Pour this mixture into the well and begin mixing the flour into the middle from the inside edges of the well. Continue incorporating flour until you have a soft dough just beyond the sticky stage. Knead the dough in the pasta machine until it is elastic. Stretch the dough in the machine, dusting with flour as needed to keep it from sticking, until the dough is 1/16 inch thick.

3. Cut the rolled-out dough into pieces approximately 12 inches long and 4 inches wide. Brush two of the pieces of dough lightly with cold water. Using a spoon or a pastry bag, place about 1 teaspoon of filling every 2 inches on one sheet of dough, forming two rows. Place a second piece of dough over the filling and press around each pocket of filling. Cut apart with a knife or a pizza cutter into 2-inch square ravioli. Repeat with the remaining dough and filling.

4. Mix the bread crumbs and ½ cup of the Parmesan together in a bowl. Beat the eggs in another bowl. Heat the oil to 375°F in a deep pan or in an electric fryer. Dip the ravioli in the egg, then into the bread crumb mixture. Deep-fry until golden brown. Drain and serve four ravioli to a plate, sprinkled with the remaining Parmesan and chopped cilantro. Garnish each serving with a tablespoon of salsa fresca.

Note: To make the pasta dough in the food processor, start by combining the eggs, oil, and chile, then add about two-thirds of the flour. Continue adding flour to form a soft dough. Knead and roll out as described above.

CORN "RISOTTO"

We call this dish "risotto" because, although it isn't made with rice and it's baked in the oven, it comes out with the same wonderful creamy texture as the Italian rice dish. As an additional southwestern touch, we serve it with a garnish of salsa fresca. It's also delicious as a side dish.

Serves 6

>   3 tablespoons unsalted butter
>   1 small onion, finely chopped
>   2 cups fresh tender corn kernels (3 to 4 ears
>   of corn)
>   ½ cup cream
>   1 tablespoon minced jalapeño chiles
>   Salt and pepper, to taste
>   ½ cup shredded Fontina cheese (2 ounces)
>   Cilantro for garnish, coarsely chopped
>   ½ cup Salsa Fresca (page 37) (optional)

1. Preheat the oven to 400°F. Melt the butter in a skillet and saute the onion until it is lightly browned. Add the corn and cook until hot, stirring often. Pour in the cream and bring to a full boil. Cook, stirring, until most of the liquid has evaporated. Add the jalapeños and season to taste with salt and pepper.

2. Pour the mixture into a shallow baking dish. Scatter the shredded cheese over the top. Bake until the cheese is melted and the corn is bubbling slightly, 5 to 8 minutes. Serve on warm plates or in pasta bowls, topped with a little salsa fresca if desired.

CORN CRÊPES
WITH SEAFOOD FILLING
AND RED CHILE CREAM SAUCE

Fresh corn kernels add sweetness to a classic French crêpe, and cornmeal adds a crunchy note as well. Note that the batter needs to rest overnight in the refrigerator.

Serves 8

Crêpe Batter
4 ears fresh corn
1 cup milk
1 cup water
4 eggs
¼ cup cornmeal
1½ cups flour
¾ teaspoon salt
¼ cup chopped chives
3 tablespoons butter, melted

Filling
4 tablespoons butter
1 pound bay scallops
½ pound raw medium-large shrimp (26 to 30 per pound), shelled and deveined
1 cup fresh or frozen corn kernels
¼ cup chopped green onion
1 teaspoon *each* chopped chives and garlic, or to taste
Salt and pepper
2 cups Red Chile Cream Sauce (page 121)
Chopped chives, for garnish

1. For the batter, cut off the top half of the corn kernels into a bowl. Scrape the cobs with the back of a knife, squeezing out the remaining milky centers of the kernels. Combine with the remaining batter ingredients in a blender or processor and blend until smooth. Chill overnight.

2. Heat a lightly buttered 8-inch crêpe pan or nonstick skillet over high heat. Cook the crêpes, using about 4 tablespoons of batter for each crêpe (16 crêpes in all).

3. Melt the remaining butter in a skillet over medium-high heat. Saute the scallops and shrimp until opaque; add the corn and green onion, and garlic and chives to taste. Correct the seasoning with salt and pepper. (Either the crêpes or the filling or both can be made ahead of time. Refrigerate the filling if keeping for more than one hour; remove from the refrigerator 15 minutes before rolling.)

4. Preheat the oven to 350°F. Mix a third of the red chile cream sauce into the seafood mixture. Spoon a little of the filling into each crêpe, roll it up, and place it in a buttered baking dish. Cover with foil and bake 10 minutes.

5. Reheat the remaining chile sauce and pour it over the crêpes. Garnish with chives.

TORTILLA "LASAGNA"

This recipe was inspired by a similar dish done by John Sedlar at his southern California restaurant St. Estèphe (see page 155). My version is a bit more hearty and robust in flavor than his.

The lasagna rounds may be made up to a day ahead and the wedges can be browned several hours ahead and then heated in the oven just before serving.

Serves 8

> 2 red bell peppers
> 3 poblano chiles
> 1 ripe avocado, halved and pitted
> 4 ounces goat cheese, room temperature
> 2 ounces cream cheese, room temperature
> 4 cloves garlic, peeled and minced
> ¼ cup minced fresh herbs (cilantro, parsley, chives)
> Salt and pepper
> 4 large (10-inch) flour tortillas

1. Roast, peel, and seed the red bell peppers and the chiles (see page 24). Set aside on paper towels to dry.

2. Peel each avocado half, slice thinly, and set aside. In an electric mixer or food processor, or with a spoon, mix the goat cheese, cream cheese, garlic, and herbs together until smooth. Add salt and pepper to taste.

3. Lay one tortilla on a cutting board and spread it with a third of the cheese mixture. Spread a second tortilla with another third of the cheese mixture and place it on top. Lay the roasted red peppers on top of the cheese. Spread a third tortilla with remaining cheese mixture, place it on top of the red peppers, and arrange the roasted poblanos on top of this third layer. Top with the fourth tortilla. Trim the edges of the stack to make a neater cylinder, if necessary.

4. Preheat the oven to 350°F. Cut the "lasagna" into 8 wedges. To cook, heat a nonstick pan or griddle over medium heat with just a few drops of oil in it. Place a wedge of lasagna in the pan and cook on both sides until golden brown. Place on a cookie sheet and bake until heated through, about 5 minutes. Serve immediately.

Note: The herbs can be varied to your personal taste. We like to serve this with a tablespoon of Salsa Fresca on the side.

WARM GOAT CHEESE
WITH RED PEPPER COULIS

Warm goat cheese has long been served in France and then in California. Usually it is served as part of a salad, but this version is served with a warm sauce and is best eaten with bread or garlic croutons.

Serves 6

Red Pepper Coulis
4 red bell peppers, roasted, peeled, and
   seeded (see page 24)
4 cloves garlic, peeled
Salt and pepper, to taste

12 ounces goat cheese (room temperature)
½ cup dry bread crumbs
1 tablespoon chopped parsley, plus more for
   garnish
2 tablespoons Parmesan cheese
2 eggs, beaten

1. For the red pepper coulis, puree the peppers and garlic together in a food processor. Season with salt and pepper and set aside.

2. Roll the goat cheese into 6 2-ounce balls. Place a ball between two pieces of parchment or waxed paper. Flatten with the back of a small frying pan or a small cake pan to about a 3½-inch round. Repeat with the remaining cheese.

3. Preheat the oven to 450°F. Mix the bread crumbs, parsley, and Parmesan together. Dip the cheese rounds in beaten egg and then into the crumb mixture. Place them on a cookie sheet and bake until hot but not melted, about 5 minutes. Meanwhile, warm the pepper coulis in a small saucepan.

4. Spoon a little pepper coulis onto warm plates. With a metal spatula, carefully place a round of cheese in the center of each plate. Garnish with additional parsley if desired.

Note: To make garlic croutons, toast ¼-inch slices cut from a baguette or other thin French loaf in a 350°F oven for 15 minutes. Rub the warm toasted croutons with a raw garlic clove impaled on a fork.

EGGPLANT, PROSCIUTTO, AND FONTINA

Although it's basically Italian, this light "small plate" fits in well in our menu. Its mild flavors make it a good foil when the rest of the meal is very spicy. Coupled with a salad, it can double as a lunch entree.

Serves 6

- 2 cloves garlic, minced
- 3 tablespoons olive oil
- 1 large eggplant, cut lengthwise into 12 slices
- 18 thin slices prosciutto
- 18 thin slices Italian fontina

1. Mix the garlic and olive oil together. Brush on both sides of each eggplant slice. Grill or broil the slices just until tender, about 2 minutes on each side.

2. Cut each grilled eggplant slice in half again lengthwise. Place four strips of eggplant overlapping on each plate. Lay 3 pieces of prosciutto across the eggplant. Lay 3 pieces of cheese over the prosciutto. Place under the broiler until the cheese is barely melted.

Note: If you don't have room under your broiler for all the plates, you can assemble and broil the portions on a sheet pan and transfer them to plates with a large spatula.

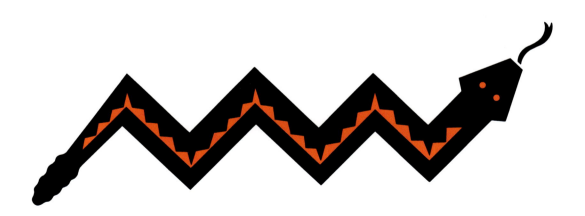

CORN AND BRIE FRITTATA
WITH AVOCADO SALSA

This can be served as an appetizer, as a luncheon main course, or as a brunch item. Served with bacon or sausage, it would also make a good breakfast dish. The avocado salsa is basically a very chunky form of guacamole. Other salsas could also be served.

Serves 8

  12 ounces Brie
  4 tablespoons butter
  1 medium onion, finely chopped
  4 jalapeño chiles, finely diced
  12 eggs
  Salt and pepper, to taste
  1½ cups cut corn, fresh or frozen
  2 cups Avocado Salsa (page 38)

1. Place the cheese in the freezer for 20 minutes to firm it up slightly. Cut into 1-inch cubes. If you prefer, scrape off some or all of the rind with a cheese plane before cutting into cubes.

2. Preheat the oven to 375°F. Melt 2 tablespoons of the butter in a skillet and saute the onion and jalapeños until soft. Let cool.

3. Beat the eggs with the salt and pepper. Stir in the corn, onion, jalapeños, and cheese. Melt the remaining butter in a 10-inch skillet (preferably nonstick and with a heatproof handle) over medium heat. Add the egg mixture and cook until the eggs are set around the edges and beginning to brown. Transfer to the oven and bake until brown and puffed, about 30 minutes.

4. Turn the frittata out onto a platter upside down and cut into 8 wedges. Serve with avocado salsa.

SONORAN SHRIMP COCKTAIL

〰〰〰〰〰〰〰

This dish was concocted for the menu by one of our talented sous chefs who really loves chiles; for him hotter is better. If you want to tone down the heat, use one chile or the other instead of one of each.

Serves 6

> 1 cup dry white wine
> 1 cup water
> 1 bay leaf
> 1 teaspoon salt
> ½ lemon, sliced
> 24 large raw unpeeled shrimp
>   (16 to 20 per pound)
> 5 medium tomatoes
> 3 tomatillos
> 6 green onions
> 1 small red onion
> 1 tablespoon roasted garlic (see page 111)
> 1 small poblano chile, roasted, peeled, and
>   seeded (see page 24)
> 1 jalapeño chile, seeded and chopped
> 2 tablespoons chopped reconstituted sun-
>   dried tomatoes
> Juice of 1 lime (2 to 3 tablespoons)
> 2 tablespoons prepared horseradish
> Salt and pepper, to taste
> 2 cups finely shredded romaine lettuce
> ½ cup coarsely chopped cilantro
> 6 lime slices

1. Bring the wine, water, bay leaf, salt and lemon to a boil in a saucepan. Add the shrimp and simmer until pink and opaque, 2 to 3 minutes. Set aside to cool in the liquid. Peel and devein, leaving the tail shells on.

2. Cut the tomatoes in half and broil them cut side up until caramelized (or if you have the grill going, grill them whole). Roast the tomatillos, green onions, and red onion under the broiler or on the grill until slightly charred. Combine the roasted vegetables, roasted garlic, poblano and jalapeño chiles, and sun-dried tomatoes in a food processor and puree. Thin with the lime juice, if needed. Season to taste with horseradish, salt, and pepper. Mix this sauce with the peeled shrimp and set aside in the refrigerator for about 2 hours.

3. Divide the shredded romaine among 6 serving dishes. Lay 4 shrimp on each plate and spoon some sauce over the top. Garnish with the chopped cilantro and lime slices. To serve in the classic shrimp cocktail style, heap the lettuce in a footed glass and arrange the shrimp so the tails hang over the edge; slit a slice of lime and press it on the rim of each glass.

Note: The sauce can be made up to 2 days ahead, so if you have the grill going one day, you can roast the vegetables and plan to serve this dish a day or two later. Of course, you can always roast the vegetables earlier in the day that you plan to serve them, but be sure to allow enough time for the sauce to rest in the refrigerator before serving.

Note: Dried tomatoes are not a traditional southwestern ingredient, but I like the flavor and texture they add to this sauce. Some are dried in the sun, others in ovens, and they vary in degree of dryness. The oil-packed version is already rehydrated and ready to use, but the dry ones need to be soaked in warm water until plump and soft, 30 minutes to an hour depending on the degree of dryness.

SALMON CAKES
AND WILTED SPINACH
WITH TOMATILLO SALSA

This is a knockoff of New England crab cakes turned southwestern. The recipe originally came to Café Terra Cotta through a line cook with a New York restaurant background. The tomatillo salsa can be made up to two days ahead.

Serves 6

Salmon Cakes
1 pound salmon filet, bones and skin
   removed
½ cup corn kernels (fresh or frozen)
1 teaspoon Dijon mustard
1 egg
1 egg yolk
1 small red bell pepper, finely chopped
2 tablespoons basil, chopped
2 cloves garlic, peeled and minced
1 tablespoon fresh lemon juice
½ cup dry bread crumbs (approximately)
Salt and pepper, to taste

3 tablespoons oil
¼ cup olive oil
1 teaspoon red chile flakes
Dash of white wine vinegar
Dash of fresh lemon juice

Salt and pepper, to taste
2 bunches spinach, cleaned and stemmed
2 cups Tomatillo Salsa (page 37)

1. Chop the salmon by hand with a knife (a processor will make it too mousse-like). Combine in a bowl with the remaining salmon cake ingredients except the bread crumbs and seasonings. Add only enough bread crumbs to take up the moisture in the mixture. Season to taste with salt and pepper.

2. Preheat the oven to 300°F. Form the salmon mixture into 12 patties (if you have a scale, each one should weigh about 2 ounces). Heat a very small amount of oil in a frying pan and brown the patties on both sides. Remove the patties to a baking sheet and bake in the oven until they don't have much give when lightly pressed, about 5 minutes.

3. Meanwhile, whisk together the olive oil, chile flakes, vinegar, and lemon juice. Season to taste. Heat this mixture in a large frying pan. Add the spinach and toss quickly just until barely wilted.

4. To serve, divide the spinach among 6 plates. Place 2 salmon patties on top of the spinach. Spoon the Tomatillo Salsa on top.

CABRILLA CAKES

Cabrilla is a sea bass found in the waters off Mexico. It has both great texture and taste. Any type of sea bass or grouper can be substituted.

Serves 8 (or 4 as an entree)

2 pounds cabrilla filet
2 medium potatoes
4 tablespoons butter
1 small onion, finely chopped
¾ cup cream
Salt and pepper, to taste
Flour

1. Bake the cabrilla in a 375°F oven until just beginning to flake, about 10 minutes. Cool and flake. Set aside.

2. Boil the potatoes until tender. Cool, peel, and grate them. Mix them with the flaked fish.

3. Melt the butter in a skillet over medium heat. Add the onion and saute until soft. Add the cream and reduce slightly. Stir into the fish and potato mixture. Season with salt and pepper to taste. (The mixture can be made up to 24 hours ahead of time and refrigerated.)

4. Form the fish mixture into 8 to 10 thick patties. Dip the patties lightly in flour and brown both sides in a lightly oiled frying pan or on a griddle. Transfer to a baking pan and bake 10 minutes at 375°F. Serve plain or drizzled with a spicy aioli (garlicky mayonnaise).

Variation: These cakes are also good topped with Salsa Fresca or Tomatillo Salsa (page 37), or served in a pool of Red Chile Cream Sauce (page 121).

SOUPS

SUMMER SQUASH SOUP

SOUTHWESTERN GAZPACHO

AVOCADO VICHYSSOISE

ROASTED EGGPLANT
AND PEPPER SOUP

TORTILLA SOUP

SMOKED ACORN SQUASH SOUP

BLACK BEAN CHILI WITH
SIRLOIN AND ASIAGO

CORN AND
YELLOW PEPPER SOUP

RICE AND PEPPER SOUP

Soups play an important part in traditional Mexican and southwestern cuisine. A bowl of soup can be a nutritious beginning to a meal, or it can be a meal in itself, especially when made with hearty, filling ingredients like *pozole* (hominy), beans, or dried meats. With abundant use of herbs and spices, even a simple vegetable soup can become a delicious main course.

Despite this tradition, and even though soups allow much room for experimentation and creativity, soup has never been an especially large category on the menu at Café Terra Cotta. We rarely offer more than two at any one time, and one of those is likely to be the Mexican-inspired Tortilla Soup that has been on our menu from the very first. In the colder months (and there are not many in Arizona), I like a hot robust soup like our Black Bean Chili or Smoked Acorn Squash Soup. During the long summer, cold soups such as Gazpacho or Avocado Vichyssoise are always popular.

Given my classical French background, many of our soups are purees. Before food processors, this type of soup was pureed in a blender or a hand-cranked food mill, which sometimes produce better results. Another option is a small hand-held blender that you insert right into the cooking pot. How finely to puree the soup, whether or not to strain it, and how fine a strainer to use, are matters of personal preference. If you want a perfectly smooth, velvety soup, use a fine strainer. You may prefer the more rustic texture of unstrained soups.

In many of my favorite soups, both hot and cold, I like the combination of chiles and cream. The silkiness of a cream-based soup develops a complexity when offset by the spiciness of chiles. Many of your favorite soups can be given a southwestern flavor with the addition of chiles or a garnish of cilantro or a dollop of salsa. Even a canned chicken stock can be spiced up by adding a jalapeño cut in half and simmering for 30 minutes.

SUMMER SQUASH SOUP

Summertime is a gardener's dream — until there is an overabundance of squashes. Use this soup to solve the problem. You can freeze it for future use; it may be slightly watery when thawed, but a few minutes of cooking will evaporate any excess liquid. Always readjust the seasoning when reheating a frozen soup.

Serves 12

½ cup olive oil
1 onion, coarsely chopped
1 carrot, coarsely chopped
3 celery stalks, coarsely chopped
1 teaspoon minced garlic
1 pound zucchini, coarsely chopped
1 pound yellow squash, coarsely chopped
1 quart Basic Chicken Stock (page 20)
1 cup dry white wine
1 teaspoon ground cumin
2 teaspoons dried oregano
Pinch of cayenne pepper
Salt and pepper, to taste
1 bunch cilantro, washed, dried, and chopped
2 cups cream
¼ pound smoked salmon, chopped
½ recipe Red Pepper Coulis (page 56)
1 cup chopped cilantro

1. Heat the olive oil in a large pot and saute the onion, carrot, celery, and garlic until soft. Add the zucchini and yellow squash. Add the chicken stock, wine, seasonings, and one bunch of cilantro. Simmer until all the vegetables are soft.

2. Puree the soup in batches. Mix in the cream. (Can be prepared to this point ahead of time.)

3. Heat the soup to serving temperature and adjust the seasonings. Garnish each serving with a few pieces of smoked salmon, a drizzle of red pepper coulis, and chopped cilantro.

SOUTHWESTERN GAZPACHO

Gazpacho is a hot weather favorite, and given Tucson and Scottsdale temperatures that means nearly year round. The addition of a chopped poblano and cilantro gives this classic dish a southwestern flair. For an additional kick add a jigger of beer to each bowl just before serving.

Serves 8

6 medium tomatoes, peeled and seeded
2 medium white onions
5 cups tomato juice
2 medium red bell peppers, seeded
2 medium green bell peppers, seeded
2 small cucumbers, peeled and seeded
1 poblano chile, seeded and deveined
¼ cup balsamic vinegar
½ cup olive oil
1 tablespoon minced garlic
1 teaspoon salt
1 teaspoon black pepper
½ teaspoon cayenne pepper
Coarsely chopped cilantro, for garnish
Sour cream, for garnish

1. Puree the tomatoes and one of the onions in a food processor or blender until smooth, adding some of the tomato juice to liquify. Dice the peppers, cucumbers, chile, and remaining onion and stir them into the puree.

2. Whisk the vinegar, oil, and garlic together in another bowl. Stir in the diced vegetables and the tomato puree. Add the balance of the tomato juice, making sure the ingredients are well blended. Whisk in the seasonings, adjusting to taste.

3. Chill and serve in soup bowls, garnished with chopped cilantro and a dollop of sour cream.

Note: Try adding some yellow bell peppers when available for extra color.

Variation: Recently at the restaurant we have begun to present this dish in a more dramatic way (see the photo opposite). Instead of mixing the diced vegetables into the tomato puree in step 1, layer a small portion of each in a juice glass, then unmold it into the center of a deep plate or a shallow soup bowl. Combine the remaining ingredients and spoon them around the vegetable "towers."

AVOCADO VICHYSSOISE

The avocado in this soup turns a traditional potato-based soup into something the French would never recognize! Because of the richness of the avocado, we can use milk instead of cream without compromising the texture.

Serves 8 to 10

1 pound potatoes, peeled and roughly cut
3 poblano chiles
4 tomatillos, husks removed
6 green onions
1 serrano chile, seeded
½ bunch cilantro, large stems removed
2 tablespoons mint leaves
2 tablespoons lime juice
1 tablespoon candied ginger, minced OR
    2 teaspoons grated fresh ginger
2 ripe avocados, peeled, seeded, and
    roughly chopped
6 to 8 cups milk
Salt and pepper
½ cup sour cream
1 teaspoon pureed chipotle chile

1. Steam or boil the potatoes until soft. Drain and let cool. Meanwhile, roast, peel, and seed the poblanos as directed on page 24. Using the same heat source, roast the tomatillos and green onions until lightly charred.

2. Combine the roasted vegetables and potatoes in a food processor or blender and puree. Add the serrano chile, cilantro, mint, lime juice, ginger, and avocado and puree until smooth, adding milk as necessary to facilitate the blending. Transfer to a bowl or storage container and thin to the desired texture with milk. Add salt and pepper to taste. Chill.

3. Taste the chilled soup for seasoning and correct if necessary. Mix the sour cream and chipotle chile together and drizzle over each bowl of soup as a garnish.

Note: Normally this soup is served cold, but it can be reheated gently and served warm. If you prefer it less spicy, leave out the chipotle cream garnish and simply garnish with a sprig of cilantro.

ROASTED EGGPLANT
AND PEPPER SOUP

Eggplant lovers will enjoy this soup. It is hearty enough to make a whole meal when combined with a salad and delicious crusty bread. This version is a smooth puree; for a more rustic, chunky soup, do not strain or puree it. You can also leave out the cream if you like.

Serves 6

 1 eggplant, peeled and sliced ¼ inch thick
 2 tablespoons olive oil
 2 red bell peppers, sliced
 ½ medium onion, sliced
 3 cloves garlic, chopped
 1 quart Basic Chicken Stock (page 20)
 2 tomatoes, seeded and chopped
 1 teaspoon black pepper
 ¾ teaspoon salt
 ¼ teaspoon cayenne
 ¼ cup cream (optional)

1. Grill or broil the eggplant slices until soft, about 2 minutes per side. Set aside.

2. Heat the oil in a large pot and saute the peppers and onion until soft. Add the garlic, stock, eggplant, and tomatoes. Bring to a boil, reduce the heat, and simmer for 15 minutes.

3. Puree the soup in batches in a food processor or blender. Pass through a coarse strainer. Season to taste with pepper, salt, and cayenne. Reheat and add the cream.

TORTILLA SOUP

Most southwestern and Mexican restaurants have their favorite recipe for a soup garnished with fried tortilla strips. This is on our menu as "Jennifer's Tortilla Soup" after one of our cooks who worked on the original recipe.

Serves 6

> 2 tablespoons olive oil
> 1 small onion, chopped
> 2 quarts Basic Chicken Stock (page 20)
> 1 teaspoon chopped garlic
> 1 bay leaf
> ½ teaspoon oregano
> 3 or 4 peppercorns
> 2 chiltepín
> 2 cups Salsa Fresca (page 37)
> Salt and pepper, to taste
> Corn oil for frying
> 4 corn tortillas, cut into strips
> 1 ripe avocado, sliced thin
> 1 lime, cut into 12 wedges
> ¾ cup Monterey jack cheese, grated

1. Heat the oil in a large pot and saute the onion until soft. Add the stock, garlic, bay leaf, oregano, peppercorns, and chiltepín and simmer for 1 hour. Puree 1½ cups of the salsa fresca and add it to the soup. Remove from the heat. Season to taste with salt and pepper.

2. Fill a deep saucepan with corn oil to a depth of 2 inches and heat to 375°F. (If you don't have an oil thermometer, heat the oil until a piece of tortilla dropped in the oil sizzles immediately, but don't let the oil start smoking.) Fry the tortilla strips until golden brown and crisp.

3. Divide the fried tortilla chips into wide soup bowls. Add 2 or 3 slices of avocado, a lime wedge, and some grated cheese to each bowl. Pour in the hot broth, add a dollop of salsa, and serve immediately, with the additional lime wedges on the side.

Note: If you prefer not to deep-fry the tortillas, brush them lightly with oil before cutting into strips and bake on a cookie sheet in a 350°F oven until dry and crisp.

SMOKED ACORN SQUASH SOUP

This is a good fall and winter soup. If you can keep the squash halves intact when scooping out the flesh, you might try serving the soup in the shells.

Serves 8

> 4 acorn squash (about 1½ pounds each), halved and seeded
> 3 tablespoons olive oil
> 1 yellow bell pepper, roasted, peeled, and seeded
> 1 carrot, coarsely chopped
> 1 onion, coarsely chopped
> 1 tablespoon chopped garlic
> 3 quarts water (approximately)
> 1 cup milk
> 1 tablespoon minced fresh thyme
> 1 tablespoon chopped fresh basil
> Lemon juice, to taste
> 8 small sprigs of thyme, for garnish

1. Smoke the squash cut side down in a wok (see page 23) about 30 minutes. (You will probably have to do this in two batches; add more wood chips if necessary when you put in the second batch of squash.) Transfer to a baking dish, cover with foil, and bake in a 350°F oven until very soft, 40 to 50 minutes. Let cool. Meanwhile, heat the oil in a large pot and saute the pepper, carrot, onion, and garlic until the onion is golden. Add 2 quarts water and simmer until the vegetables are tender.

2. When the squash is cooled, scoop out the pulp and add it to the vegetables. Puree until very smooth, adding more water as needed.

3. Add milk to reach a desired consistency. Stir in the herbs and lemon juice to taste. Refrigerate if not serving immediately. Heat gently to serving temperature and garnish with a thyme sprig.

Note: Chicken stock could be substituted for all or part of the water in this recipe.

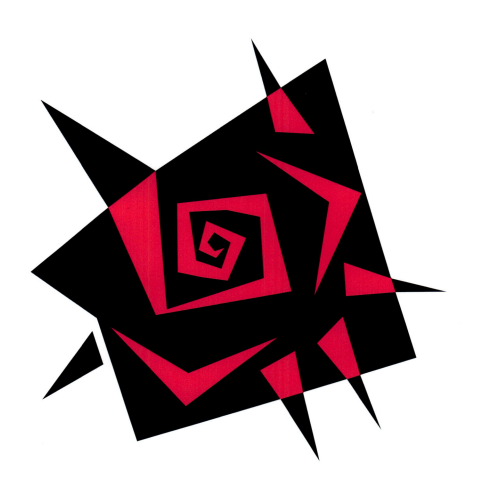

BLACK BEAN CHILI
WITH SIRLOIN AND ASIAGO

This recipe is from the original Café Terra Cotta menu and will probably remain there forever. This dish maintains its popularity even when the temperature in Arizona climbs over the 100-degree mark. Note that you have to soak the beans overnight, or use the quick soak method.

Grilling the meat and adding it at the end rather than stewing it together with the beans keeps the meat more distinguishable. Also, this way we can serve the chili by itself to vegetarians.

Serves 8

    1 pound dried black beans
    1 tablespoon whole cumin seeds
    ½ teaspoon cayenne
    2 teaspoons paprika
    1 tablespoon dried oregano leaves
    1 small pasilla chile
    2 tablespoons olive oil
    1 large yellow onion, chopped
    1 teaspoon salt, plus more to taste
    1 chipotle chile, chopped
    4 cloves of garlic, chopped
    4 large ripe tomatoes, peeled, seeded, and
        chopped
    1 medium green bell pepper, seeded and
        chopped
    1 bay leaf
    1 pound sirloin steak
    ½ cup chopped cilantro
    ½ cup Salsa Fresca (page 37)
    ½ cup grated aged asiago cheese

1. Sort through the beans and discard any stones. Rinse well. Soak overnight, or use the quick soak procedure on page 25.

2. Toast the cumin seeds, cayenne, paprika, and oregano lightly in a large dry skillet over a medium flame. Do not let them burn. Remove and set aside.

3. Remove the stem, seeds, and veins from the pasilla chile and grind the chile to a powder in a spice grinder or blender.

4. Heat the oil in the same skillet and saute the onion until softened. Add 1 teaspoon salt and the chipotle chile, ground pasilla chile, toasted spices, garlic, tomatoes, and bell pepper and cook together for about 15 minutes.

5. Drain the beans and place them in a large pot. Add the contents of the skillet and the bay leaf. Add water to cover by 2 to 3 inches. Bring to a boil, reduce the heat, and simmer until the beans are soft, 1½ to 3 hours.

6. When the beans are cooked, season to taste with salt. Grill the steak, cut it into cubes, and stir into the beans along with the cilantro. Serve in bowls, garnishing each serving with a tablespoon of salsa fresca and a tablespoon of grated cheese.

CORN AND YELLOW PEPPER SOUP
WITH MARJORAM PESTO

Here's another use for that ever-popular southwestern ingredient, corn. The marjoram pesto is unusual, but after trial and error we found that marjoram balanced the sweetness of the corn far better than the more biting flavor of basil. Any leftover pesto would be good on pasta or sliced tomatoes.

Serves 8

    1 cup (loosely packed) fresh marjoram
    1 cup (loosely packed) fresh cilantro
    1 cup parsley
    2 medium garlic cloves
    ½ cup plus 2 tablespoons olive oil
    2 teaspoons grated Parmesan cheese
    1 tablespoon lime juice
    Salt and pepper, to taste
    1 medium onion, sliced
    6 ears fresh corn, kernels removed *OR*
        2 10-ounce boxes of frozen corn,
        thawed
    2 cups Basic Chicken Stock (page 20)
    2 medium yellow bell peppers, roasted,
        peeled, and seeded
    1 teaspoon roasted garlic (see page 111)
    1 cup cream

1. For the pesto, chop the marjoram, cilantro, parsley, and garlic together in a food processor until thoroughly blended. Slowly add ½ cup of the olive oil. Stir in the cheese and lime juice and season to taste with salt and pepper.

2. Heat the remaining 2 tablespoons oil in a large saucepan and saute the onion until golden. Add the corn and stock to cover and simmer for 5 minutes. Puree the corn mixture with the roasted peppers and garlic and the remaining chicken stock.

3. Return the soup to the pot, add the cream, and bring to a gentle boil, stirring lightly. Season to taste with salt and pepper. Drizzle each serving of soup with the marjoram pesto.

RICE AND PEPPER SOUP

This light, healthful soup uses bell peppers for a mild flavor. To add heat, add a few serrano chiles. For a vegetarian version, use a vegetable stock in place of the chicken or beef stock.

Serves 6

 6 tablespoons olive oil
 3 cups finely chopped onion (about 3
   medium onions)
 2 cups chopped peeled carrots (about 2
   medium carrots)
 6 cloves garlic, chopped
 7 cups Basic Chicken Stock (page 20) or
   beef stock
 ½ cup uncooked long-grain rice
 ½ cup dry sherry
 2 red bell peppers, seeded and julienned
 2 green bell peppers, seeded and julienned
 Salt and pepper, to taste

1. Heat the olive oil in a soup pot over low heat. Add the onions, carrots, and garlic and cook, covered, until the vegetables are tender and slightly colored, about 25 minutes. Stir occasionally.

2. Uncover the pot, add the stock, and bring to a boil over high heat. Reduce the heat to low, cover, and simmer for 20 minutes.

3. Pour the soup through a strainer, pressing hard with the back of a spoon to extract as much flavor as possible (but don't push the vegetables through the strainer — this is supposed to be a broth, not a puree). Discard the solids and return the broth to the pot. Add the rice, sherry, peppers, and salt and pepper to taste. Simmer partially covered until the rice is tender, about 25 minutes. Correct the seasoning and serve immediately.

good —
2 serranos good "heat"

SALADS

CITRONETTE DRESSING

BALSAMIC JALAPEÑO
VINAIGRETTE

TANGY CHEESE-STUFFED QUAIL
WITH MANGO-CHILE SALSA

SMOKED CORNISH HEN WITH
SUNFLOWER SPROUTS
AND SCALLIONS

STEAK SALAD WITH SAUTEED
RED AND YELLOW PEPPERS

MUSSEL SALAD WITH
CORN AND RED PEPPER

LIME-GINGER CITRONETTE

WARM CABBAGE SALAD

SPINACH SALAD WITH
FIGS AND JICAMA

CHILE-ORANGE VINAIGRETTE

GRILLED TUNA SALAD

ARIZONA COLESLAW

MUSHROOM, JARLSBERG,
AND PARSLEY SALAD

SPICY CHICKEN SALAD

CHAYOTE SALAD

Salads have come a long way since the days of the iceberg wedge and thousand island dressing. Not only has the content of salads changed, but their role has also been modified. Salads, in the past, were generally a collection of greens with a basic dressing, served as a side to the entree, before the entree (American style) or afterward (European style). Today, with the popularity of eating light, the main dish salad has come into its own with a wide variety of imaginative ingredients including items such as steak that were primarily used for entrees.

I am very much a part of the trend towards main dish salads. When I'm not particularly hungry, an interesting salad just hits the spot. For this reason, most of the salad recipes I've included can be substituted for either appetizers or entrees. You will find a steak salad, a quail salad, and a duck salad.

You will also notice in many of the salad recipes, I use a citronette dressing or balsamic vinegar. Even when I call for a vinaigrette, the proportions play down the acidity of the vinegar or citrus. The reason is the negative effect of these acids when drinking wine. If, like me, you like a glass of wine with your meal, you will want to keep the acidity of the dressing to a minimum. Additionally, note that I do not hesitate to flavor my dressings with chiles, prickly pear syrup, and the like.

As a final comment, please take advantage of the multitude of fancy salad greens that are becoming readily available in most chain grocery stores today. Radicchio, oakleaf, arugula, mâche, frisee, many available as baby lettuces, add to the flavor and complexity of a salad. While not wishing any harm to the iceberg lettuce industry, I think there are far too many alternatives available to revert back to iceberg wedges.

CITRONETTE DRESSING

Citron is the French word for lemon. We use it in our standard "house" dressing on our mixed green salad and on other salad specials from time to time. Lemon is milder than vinegar and therefore is less likely to clash with a wine served during the salad course. The dressing can be made in moderate quantities and kept in the refrigerator for use during the week.

Makes 2 cups

½ cup lemon juice
1½ cups olive oil
4 cloves garlic, peeled and minced
½ tablespoon Dijon mustard
½ teaspoon salt
½ teaspoon pepper

Whisk all the ingredients together. Adjust the seasoning to taste.

BALSAMIC JALAPEÑO VINAIGRETTE

This is another one of our standard dressings, used in the spinach salad on page 91 and the cheese-stuffed quail on page 84. Like lemon juice, balsamic vinegar has a mild acidity that is gentler on the taste buds than other vinegars.

Makes 1¼ cups

¼ cup balsamic vinegar
2 jalapeño chiles, finely chopped
1 teaspoon minced garlic
1 cup olive oil
Salt and pepper, to taste

Mix the vinegar, chiles, and garlic. Whisk in the oil and season with salt and pepper.

TANGY CHEESE-STUFFED QUAIL
WITH MANGO-CHILE SALSA

Quail are abundant in Arizona, but they are thought by most residents to be too cute to eat. We find they are more appealing to our many tourists. I like them because they make a light entree salad course.

Serves 6

¼ pound goat cheese
¼ pound blue cheese
2 tablespoons chopped cilantro
2 medium garlic cloves, minced
6 quail
6 to 8 cups assorted baby lettuces
½ pint fresh raspberries or blackberries
½ cup Balsamic Jalapeño Vinaigrette
  (page 83)

Mango-Chile Salsa
1 large or 2 medium ripe mangoes, peeled,
  seeded, and diced (about 2 cups)
½ cup chopped cilantro
1 dried ancho chile, soaked (see page 25),
  seeded, and chopped
1 small red bell pepper, seeded and chopped
½ teaspoon chopped garlic
1 jalapeño chile, chopped (with seeds)
Salt and pepper, to taste
Lime juice, to taste

1. Preheat the oven to 400°F. Combine the cheeses in a mixing bowl and beat with a spoon until well blended. Mix in the chopped cilantro and garlic. Form into 6 balls and place one inside each quail cavity. If you have the grill going, grill the quail until nicely marked, then place them in the oven to bake for 20 minutes. If not using a grill, bake the quail for 20 minutes, then run them under the broiler until golden brown.

2. While the quail cook, combine the salsa ingredients. Season to taste with lime juice, salt, and pepper.

3. Place a handful of greens on each plate like a nest and spoon salsa into the nests. Sprinkle fresh berries on the plate and place a quail on top of the salsa. Drizzle the salads with the vinaigrette and serve.

SMOKED CORNISH HEN
WITH SUNFLOWER SPROUTS
AND SCALLIONS

We use sunflower sprouts grown in Arizona. If they are not available, any combination of lettuces may be used as a bed for the meat.

Serves 4

2 Cornish hens
Salt and pepper

Dressing
¾ cup olive oil
¼ cup lemon juice
2 tablespoons dry vermouth
2 teaspoons champagne or Dijon mustard
¼ teaspoon grated ginger
Salt and pepper, to taste

4 cups sunflower sprouts
2 medium tomatoes, sliced
4 scallions, sliced

1. Season the hens inside and out with salt and pepper. Smoke in a wok (see page 23) for 20 minutes, then transfer to a 400°F oven and roast until the thigh juices run clear, about 20 minutes.

2. Mix the dressing ingredients together and set aside. Arrange the sunflower sprouts on plates with tomato slices overlapping along one edge.

3. Separate the legs and wings from the hens. Split and bone the breasts and slice the halves crosswise. Toss all the parts gently in the dressing. Arrange a leg, a wing, and a quarter of the breast slices on each salad and drizzle any remaining dressing over the top. Garnish with sliced scallions.

Note: This dish is very flexible when it comes to timing; you can serve it with the hens right out of the oven, or cooled to room temperature, or somewhere in between, or even cooked a day ahead of time and refrigerated — whatever is convenient.

STEAK SALAD
WITH SAUTEED RED AND YELLOW PEPPERS

This main-dish salad is a good way to eat meat during summer in the Southwest, especially when a whole steak might be too much. Of course, it is also a good way to use any leftover grilled steak.

Serves 6

> 1 medium red bell pepper, seeded and julienned
> 1 medium yellow bell pepper, seeded and julienned
> Olive oil
> Salt and pepper, to taste
> 1½ pounds flank steak, trimmed
> 6 cups assorted baby lettuces
> ½ cup Citronette Dressing (page 83)
> ¼ cup chopped cilantro
> ½ teaspoon ground chiltepín or hot chile flakes

1. Saute the peppers in a little olive oil until soft. Season with salt and pepper and set aside.

2. Grill or broil the flank steak medium rare, or to taste. Meanwhile, toss the lettuce in a bowl with half the dressing and arrange on salad plates. Slice the grilled steak thinly on the diagonal (against the grain). Combine in the same bowl with the peppers, cilantro, chiltepín, and remaining dressing and toss to coat evenly. Divide the mixture among the four plates and drizzle any remaining dressing over the salads. Serve at room temperature.

MUSSEL SALAD
WITH CORN AND RED PEPPER

My fondness for mussels comes from having spent a lot of time in Normandy during my trips to France. Of course, we don't have mussels in the desert, so we rely on purveyors to fly them in from northern waters whenever possible.

Serves 4

> 2 pounds mussels (about 4 dozen small)
> 2 teaspoons chopped garlic
> 2 tablespoons minced shallots
> 6 sprigs parsley, chopped
> 4 tablespoons butter
> Salt and pepper, to taste
> 1 cup white wine
> 1 head romaine lettuce
> ½ cup Citronette Dressing (page 83),
>   with an added pinch of oregano
> 2 cups fresh corn kernels (4 ears), cut off the
>   cob and blanched, or frozen corn kernels
> 2 medium red bell peppers, roasted, peeled,
>   seeded (see page 24), and chopped
> 1 poblano chile, roasted, peeled, seeded,
>   and chopped
> ½ cup coarsely chopped cilantro (optional)

1. Scrub the mussels well and remove any beards. Place the mussels in a saucepan with the garlic, shallots, parsley, and butter. Season with salt and pepper. Add 1 inch of wine and bring to a boil. Cover and simmer for 3 minutes or until all the shells are open. Discard any mussels that don't open. Cool and shuck the mussels and discard the shells.

2. Discard the heavy outer leaves of the romaine and cut the inner leaves into fine shreds (chiffonade). Toss lightly with some of the dressing and place on salad plates. Toss the mussels, corn, red pepper, and poblano in the remaining dressing and place the mixture on the chiffonade. Sprinkle with cilantro as desired.

Variation: Shrimp could be substituted for the mussels, although the flavor and texture will be different.

Variation: Replace the basic dressing with Lime-Ginger Citronette (below).

LIME-GINGER CITRONETTE

Makes 1¼ cups

> 2 ounces lime juice
> 1 teaspoon crystallized ginger pieces
> 1 teaspoon minced lime zest
> ½ teaspoon minced garlic
> 1 teaspoon honey
> 1 cup olive oil
> Salt and pepper, to taste

Combine the lime juice and ginger in a blender and blend until the ginger is cut into little pieces. Do not strain. Transfer to a bowl and mix in the lime zest, garlic, and honey. Whisk in the oil and season with salt and pepper.

WARM CABBAGE SALAD

This salad is colorful and tasty. Serve it as is for a salad, with good crusty bread or toast points, or omit the goat cheese and use it as a side dish with any roasted meat or fowl.

Serves 8

    8 ounces goat cheese
    ¼ cup vegetable oil
    4 garlic cloves, minced
    1 medium red cabbage, cut into ¼-inch slices
    ¼ cup red wine vinegar
    ¾ cup toasted pecans
    6 thick slices mesquite-smoked bacon,
        well cooked and chopped

1. Divide the goat cheese into 8 portions. Form each portion into a ball and flatten it between waxed paper into a disc about ¼ inch thick. Set aside at room temperature.

2. Heat the oil and garlic in a saute pan. Add the sliced cabbage and saute until it begins to soften. Add the vinegar and stir to deglaze the pan. Season with salt and pepper.

3. Remove from the heat and mix in the pecans and bacon. Arrange on plates, with a round of goat cheese on top of each salad.

SPINACH SALAD
WITH FIGS AND JICAMA

This is a basic recipe for which I have many variations. Adding pitted dates or substituting grilled shiitake mushrooms for the figs are just two of many possibilities.

Serves 8

- 1 pound spinach, stems removed, well washed and dried
- ½ cup Balsamic Jalapeño Vinaigrette (page 83)
- 1 cup dried Calimyrna or fresh black mission figs, quartered
- 1 small jicama, skin removed, cut in strips (about 4 cups)
- 1 red bell pepper, seeded and cut in thin strips

Toss the spinach in a bowl with half the dressing and arrange on salad plates. Toss the figs and jicama together with the remaining dressing in the same bowl and place on top of the spinach. Garnish with red pepper strips and drizzle any dressing remaining in the bowl over the salad.

Variations

◆ Cooking the jicama on the grill brings out a surprisingly sweet and smoky flavor. Grill it in large slices and cut them into strips before adding to the salad.

◆ For a savory rather than sweet flavor, substitute grilled shiitake mushrooms for the figs.

◆ Radishes and blue cheese make another good topping for a spinach salad in place of the figs, jicama, and red pepper. Toss the spinach in the dressing, then scatter the radishes and cheese over the top.

◆ Replace the figs with peeled and seeded orange slices and dress with Chile-Orange Vinaigrette (below).

CHILE-ORANGE VINAIGRETTE

Makes 1½ cups

- ¼ cup red wine vinegar
- ¼ cup orange juice
- 1 jalapeño chile, finely chopped
- 1 teaspoon minced garlic
- ½ cup Dijon mustard
- 1 cup olive oil
- Salt and pepper, to taste

Mix the vinegar, juice, chile, garlic, and mustard together in a bowl. Whisk in the oil and season with salt and pepper.

GRILLED TUNA SALAD

This recipe is not specifically southwestern, other than the fact that tuna is found in southwestern U.S. and Mexican waters. The salad is really a version of *salade nicoise* but without Nicoise olives and using fresh grilled tuna.

Serves 4

Basil Vinaigrette
2 tablespoons red wine vinegar
6 tablespoons olive oil
¼ cup basil leaves, julienned
1 clove garlic, minced
Salt and pepper

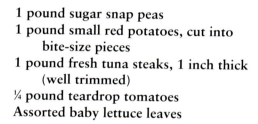

1 pound sugar snap peas
1 pound small red potatoes, cut into
    bite-size pieces
1 pound fresh tuna steaks, 1 inch thick
    (well trimmed)
¼ pound teardrop tomatoes
Assorted baby lettuce leaves

1. Whisk the vinaigrette ingredients together and adjust the seasoning to taste.

2. Steam the sugar snap peas for 2 minutes and refresh in ice water. Steam the potatoes just until tender, about 4 minutes. Refresh in ice water. Sprinkle with salt and pepper and toss lightly with the peas in a little of the vinaigrette.

3. Grill or broil the tuna about 4 minutes per side. Cut into 1-inch chunks. Add the tuna (warm or at room temperature) to the vegetables and toss with the remaining dressing. Arrange the tuna and vegetables on a platter or individual salad plates lined with baby lettuces.

Variation: Add 2 tablespoons prickly pear syrup to the dressing.

ARIZONA COLESLAW
WITH AVOCADO AND JICAMA

A refreshing change to an old salad. Cabbage never tasted so good.

Serves 8

½ **head green cabbage, shredded (6 to 8 cups)**
¼ **head red cabbage, shredded (about 3 cups)**
1 **cup chopped cilantro**
2 **tablespoons lime juice**
6 **tablespoons vegetable oil**
Salt and pepper, to taste
2 **avocados, sliced**
½ **jicama, peeled, sliced, and cut into triangles**
2 **tomatoes, sliced**

1. Toss the green and red cabbage in a bowl with the cilantro, lime juice, and oil. Season with salt and pepper. Let stand about 10 minutes.

2. Heap the coleslaw in the middle of a platter or individual salad plates. Garnish the outside edges with avocado slices, jicama triangles, and tomato slices.

Variation: Add ½ teaspoon ground cumin when mixing the coleslaw.

MUSHROOM, JARLSBERG, AND PARSLEY SALAD

~~~~~~~~

This salad gets a refreshing, "nutty" taste from the combination of mushrooms and cheese. It is a nice change from the typical green salad.

Serves 6

 1 pound mushrooms, sliced
 ¼ pound Jarlsberg cheese, shredded
 ½ cup minced parsley
 ¼ cup lemon juice
 ¾ cup olive oil
 Salt and pepper, to taste

6 large red lettuce leaves
Lemon slices, for garnish

Toss the mushrooms, cheese, parsley, lemon juice, and oil together. Season to taste. Serve each portion on a red lettuce leaf and garnish with a twisted lemon slice.

Note: This salad should be dressed no longer than ½ hour before serving so that the mushrooms retain their best color and texture.

SPICY CHICKEN SALAD

~~~~~~~~~

Chicken salad is a favorite dish for most people. Some styles can be used in sandwiches as well as an entree or luncheon dish. Your imagination is the only limitation on variations.

Serves 8

    3 chicken breasts, boned and skinned
        (6 half breasts)
    Oil
    3 red bell peppers, roasted, peeled, and
        seeded (page 24)
    2 poblano chiles, roasted, peeled, and seeded
    ½ cup chopped cilantro
    ½ cup olive oil (approximately)
    1 teaspoon ground chiltepín
    Salt and pepper, to taste
    4 to 6 cups sunflower sprouts or assorted
        baby lettuces

1. Lay the chicken breasts on a baking sheet lined with parchment paper. Brush with a little oil and cover with another sheet of parchment. Bake in a 350°F oven about 10 minutes. It is most important not to overcook the chicken. Don't forget that it will continue to cook when first taken out of the oven so it should be the slightest bit underdone. Cool.

2. Cut the roasted red peppers and poblanos into long strips. Place them in a bowl. Cut the chicken into long strips and add it to the peppers.

3. Mix in the cilantro, oil, and chiltepín. Season with salt and pepper. Serve with a handful of sunflower sprouts or baby lettuces on the side of the plate.

Variation: Grill or broil 8 green onions until toasty brown. Chop and add to the salad along with 2 minced cloves garlic, the juice of 1 lime, and 2 tablespoons Dijon mustard.

CHAYOTE SALAD

Chayote is a vegetable that can be served hot as a side dish or, in this case, marinated in a salad. Try it in recipes as a substitute for zucchini or yellow squash.

Serves 6

 3 chayotes
 2 tablespoons lime juice
 6 tablespoons oil
 ½ cup chopped cilantro
 Salt and pepper, to taste
 1 white onion, thinly sliced
 2 tomatoes, sliced or cut into wedges
 ½ cup pitted black olives

1. Steam the whole, unpeeled chayotes until tender. Cool completely. Peel and slice (include the seeds or remove them as you prefer). Pour the lime juice, oil, and cilantro over the slices in a bowl. Season with salt and pepper. Let marinate about 15 minutes.

2. Pour boiling water over the sliced onion and let it sit 5 minutes. Drain and rinse with cold water.

3. Arrange the chayote slices on a serving platter or on individual plates. Top with onions, tomato wedges, and olives. Drizzle any dressing remaining in the bowl over the top.

ENTREES

SHRIMP STUFFED WITH GOAT CHEESE

SHRIMP WITH CHIPOTLE CHILE

GRILLED SHRIMP WITH ACHIOTE

SCALLOPS IN ADOBO

SALMON WITH MINTED SALSA

PAILLARD OF FISH WITH
SALSA BEURRE BLANC

SEA BASS WITH PUMPKIN SEED SALSA

CHICKEN WITH CUCUMBER-
CILANTRO BEURRE BLANC

CHICKEN BREASTS WITH ROASTED
GARLIC-GOAT CHEESE SAUCE

GRILLED CHICKEN WITH CALABACITAS

CHICKEN BREAST
AND JARLSBERG SANDWICH

QUAIL IN ESCABECHE WITH MOLE VERDE

DUCK BREAST WITH MOLE SAUCE

BAKED STUFFED POBLANO CHILES

MEAT LOAF WITH
YUCATECAN CHILE SAUCE

FILET MIGNON WITH RED
CHILE CREAM SAUCE

RIB EYE STEAK WITH BARBECUE SAUCE

DRIED CHERRY-CHIPOTLE LAMB CHOPS

LAMB CHOPS WITH TEQUILA AND HONEY

SMOKED PORK WITH WHITE BEAN CHILI

PORK WITH APRICOT CHUTNEY

PENNE WITH THREE CHEESES

Historically, entrees were the focal point of a meal. Menus were designed around the entree; appetizers and desserts were tacked on, often as an afterthought. Not anymore. The increasing popularity of "grazing" and the focus on appetizers by today's creative chefs have made entrees more of a menu peer than a centerpiece.

A second trend that has had a great effect on traditional entrees, both in home cooking and on the restaurant scene, is the avoidance by many consumers of red meat. Whether the decline is relative or absolute is academic. The reality is that interest in "white meat" (pork, fowl, veal) and non-meat (fish, shellfish, and vegetarian entrees) has increased significantly.

Still, most people want red meat every so often. When they order it they expect it to be a great piece of meat. I have found that in the restaurant the best and safest path is to buy Certified Angus Beef or CAB. Despite all the discussions and lessons on "marbling," fat content, grades, and cuts of beef, the fact remains that meat can be a difficult purchase for the average cook. CAB steaks are becoming available in most communities and are usually featured at better restaurants. If you can find them, I definitely recommend them. If not, seek out the best butcher shop you can and ask for the best they can provide.

The problem with the growing interest in fish, veal, pork, and fowl is that by themselves these meats are not very flavorful. They have always relied on sauces and accompaniments to add flavor. Fortunately, this is where contemporary southwestern cuisine really shines. Instead of chicken with gravy, at Café Terra Cotta your chicken breast is going to be accompanied by a garlic-goat cheese sauce. Pork tenderloin is smoked, or marinated in *adobado* (a mixture of lime juice, chile, and sugar) and accompanied by an apricot-chile chutney. Instead of plain old lemon butter, your fish might be served with a cucumber and cilantro sauce, or avocado salsa, or roasted peppers and a corn and pumpkin seed salsa. Even your traditional steak comes with a robust cream sauce based on dried ancho chiles. Will you remember these flavors? You'd better believe it.

SHRIMP STUFFED WITH HERBED GOAT CHEESE

This recipe has been on the Café Terra Cotta menu since the day it opened and has become a signature dish. The key to its popularity is probably the cream cheese mixed with the goat cheese, giving the stuffing a milder taste than all goat cheese.

The sauce in this dish is simply our basic Fresh Tomato Salsa recipe, cooked down to the runny state the French call a *coulis*.

Serves 4

    1 pound large shrimp (16 to 20 per pound),
        butterflied (see Note)
    4 ounces goat cheese
    4 ounces cream cheese
    1 medium clove garlic, minced
    1 tablespoon cream
    4 tablespoons chopped cilantro
    Salt and pepper, to taste
    2 tablespoons olive oil
    4 medium tomatoes, peeled, seeded, and
        chopped
    1 tablespoon chopped jalapeño chile
    Juice of one lime

1. Preheat the oven to 350°F. Bake the shrimp until barely firm, about 2 minutes. Remove and cool slightly.

2. Mix the goat cheese, cream cheese, garlic, cream, and half the cilantro together and season with salt and pepper. Pipe the cheese mixture onto the butterflied part of each shrimp with a pastry bag, or spread it on thickly with a knife.

3. Turn the oven to 400°F and return the stuffed shrimp to bake for about 3 more minutes, or until the meat is opaque. Meanwhile, heat the oil in a skillet and cook the tomatoes, covered, until they exude their juice, about 5 minutes. Add the remaining cilantro, jalapeño, and salt, pepper, and lime juice to taste. Cook, uncovered, until the moisture has almost evaporated, leaving just enough for a runny texture.

4. Spoon the tomato coulis onto warm plates and serve the stuffed shrimp on top.

Note: To butterfly shrimp, remove all but the last section of shell; cut deeply along the outside, cutting almost but not all the way through. Remove the vein near the outer edge. When the shrimp cook, the tail end will curl up.

Variation: These shrimp may also be served room temperature as an hors d'oeuvre.

SAUTEED SHRIMP
WITH CHIPOTLE CHILE
AND GREEN ONIONS

One of our alumni chefs came up with this dish when we were trying to diversify our combinations of shrimp and southwestern ingredients. It is a quick and easy recipe that can be served alone or in a bell pepper half of any color.

Serves 6

- 2 tablespoons olive oil
- 3 cloves garlic, minced
- 1½ pounds medium-large shrimp (26 to 30 per pound), peeled and deveined
- 1 bunch green onions, sliced (including most of the green)

- 1 tablespoon minced chipotle chile
- ½ cup white wine
- 2 small tomatoes, peeled, seeded, and chopped
- Salt and pepper, to taste
- 2 tablespoons unsalted butter

Heat the oil and garlic over medium heat. Add the shrimp, green onions, and chipotle and cook just until the shrimp turn pink. Add the wine and stir 1 minute. Add the chopped tomatoes and season with salt and pepper. Stir in the butter just before serving.

GRILLED SHRIMP
WITH ACHIOTE

~~~~~~~~~~

The achiote marinade in this recipe gives a subtle yin-yang tangy and sweet flavor to the shrimp. The orange juice provides sweetness and some acidity, while the achiote gives an earthy, tart flavor to balance. This marinade is also very good on pork or chicken.

Serves 8

Achiote Marinade
¼ cup achiote paste (see page 13)
2 cups orange juice
1 teaspoon chopped garlic
1 tablespoon olive oil
1 tablespoon brown sugar
Pinch of ground cumin
Pinch of ground coriander
Pinch of oregano
Salt and pepper, to taste

~~~~

2½ pounds large raw shrimp (16 to 20
   per pound), in the shell

1. Mix the marinade ingredients together. Add the shrimp and marinate 3 hours to overnight in the refrigerator.

2. Remove the shrimp from the marinade and skewer through the shells. Grill until the meat is opaque and serve over Arroz Verde (page 117).

Variation: There are both advantages and disadvantages to grilling shrimp in the shell. The shells help hold in the moisture, but keep some of the grilled flavor away from the meat. If your shrimp need deveining, you can slit open the outer curve of each shell to get at the veins and leave the shells otherwise intact. On the other hand, if you prefer not to have to deal with the shells at the table, remove all but the last section and the tail shell before marinating. Be careful not to grill peeled shrimp over too hot a fire, or they will overcook quickly and dry out.

SCALLOPS IN ADOBO

Adobo is the general name for chile or chile-tomato sauces heavily spiked with vinegar and/or citrus juices and spices. If you want to serve this with wine, be careful not to overdo the acid ingredients; otherwise, serve with beer.

Serves 4

Adobo
4 ancho chiles
2 teaspoons chopped garlic
¼ teaspoon ground cumin
½ teaspoon dried oregano
¼ teaspoon dried marjoram
¼ teaspoon ground cinnamon
3 tablespoons vinegar
½ cup orange juice
½ teaspoon salt

1 pound sea scallops
2 tablespoons olive oil
2 cups corn kernels, fresh (if available)
    or frozen

3 roasted and peeled poblano chiles
    (see page 24), cut into strips
2 bunches green onions, sliced
4 tomatoes, peeled, seeded, and chopped
Salt and pepper, to taste
½ recipe Arroz Verde (page 117)

1. Soak the ancho chiles for 1 hour in hot water. Drain and save the water. Seed the chiles and put them in a blender with the rest of the adobo ingredients. Blend until smooth, adding chile water as needed. Transfer to a bowl, toss the scallops in the adobo, and refrigerate for 4 hours.

2. Lift the scallops out of the adobo, letting the excess fall off. Heat the olive oil over high heat in a skillet and saute the scallops until seared, about 1 minute per side. Add the corn, poblanos, green onions, and tomatoes. Stir until the scallops are cooked, approximately 4 minutes. Correct the seasoning and serve over the green rice.

GRILLED SALMON
WITH MINTED SALSA

The salsa in this recipe is partly pureed and partly chunky to provide the proper texture.

Serves 8

4 medium tomatoes, peeled
1 small yellow onion, sliced
1 jalapeño chile, coarsely chopped
6 green onions, chopped
2 tablespoons finely shredded mint
2 teaspoons chopped garlic
Salt and pepper, to taste
8 salmon filets, 6 ounces each
½ cup sour cream (room temperature)

1. Place 2 of the tomatoes, the onion, and the jalapeño in boiling water and cook until soft, about 5 minutes. Drain and puree in a blender or food processor. Dice the remaining tomatoes and combine with the puree. Add the green onion, mint, and garlic and season to taste with salt and pepper.

2. Grill or broil the salmon until barely opaque, about 4 minutes per side. Warm the salsa and pour it over the salmon filets. Drizzle with sour cream.

PAILLARD OF FRESH FISH
WITH SALSA BEURRE BLANC

A "paillard" is something pounded very thin. In this case it is fish. You can also make paillards out of chicken breasts.

Serves 6

> 2 pounds firm-fleshed fish steaks (marlin, tuna, swordfish, or salmon)
> ¼ cup white wine
> ¼ cup wine vinegar
> ½ tablespoon minced shallots
> ¾ cup butter
> ⅓ cup Salsa Fresca (page 37), or to taste
> Salt and pepper, to taste

1. Partially freeze the fish and slice it across the grain about ½ inch thick. Pound with a mallet, meat pounder, or rolling pin to an even thickness of about ⅛ inch.

2. Combine the wine, vinegar, and shallots in a saucepan. Bring to a boil and reduce to 2 table-spoons of liquid. Remove the pan from the heat and whisk in the butter bit by bit. Add the salsa and heat slightly. Correct the seasoning with salt and pepper. Keep warm in a water bath if not serving right away.

3. Place the fish paillards on a cookie sheet with sides that can go under a broiler. Broil about 4 inches from the heat for 2 minutes. Transfer to warm plates and serve immediately, topped with the sauce.

Note: Beurre blanc sauces cannot be reheated too much or the butter simply melts and does not retain its creamy texture. A bath of hot (not boiling) water is best for keeping the sauce at serving temperature.

Variation: Omit the beurre blanc and serve the paillards with Avocado Salsa (page 38).

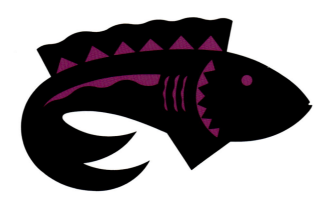

Sea Bass with Peppers
and Pumpkin Seed Salsa

〰〰〰〰〰〰

This sauce will work with grilled, broiled, or baked fish; use whichever technique is most convenient for you. My gauge for doneness is 8 minutes per inch of thickness. This is slightly underdone, but not rare. Use your own judgment if you prefer your fish more cooked.

Serves 6

1 cup corn kernels, fresh (if available) or frozen
6 tomatillos, diced
1 cup toasted pumpkin seeds
1 poblano chile, roasted, peeled, seeded, and chopped
Juice of 1 lime
½ teaspoon cumin
Salt and pepper, to taste
6 Chilean sea bass filets (or other flaky fish), 6 to 8 ounces each
1 red bell pepper, roasted, peeled, seeded, and cut into strips

1. For the salsa, combine the corn, tomatillos, pumpkin seeds, and poblano chile. Season with the lime juice, cumin, salt, and pepper. Set aside in the refrigerator for 2 hours, if time permits.

2. Season the fish lightly with salt and pepper and grill, broil, or bake it until done to your taste. Serve with the salsa and garnish with roasted pepper strips.

Note: This salsa is best if it is done about 2 hours ahead. It will keep overnight, but will have a slightly softer texture.

GRILLED CHICKEN (OR FISH)
WITH CUCUMBER-CILANTRO
BEURRE BLANC

This is one of the recipes from the first Café Terra Cotta menu. The sauce can be served on chicken or fish as described here, or with pork or veal. The cucumbers add not only a subtle herbaceous taste, but also a crunchy texture, and a beautiful shade of green as they glisten in the buttery sauce.

Serves 4

> 1 cup oil
> 1 or 2 serrano or jalapeño chiles,
>   coarsely chopped
> ½ cup cilantro, coarsely chopped
> 1 teaspoon salt
> 4 whole chicken breasts OR 4 fish filets,
>   6 to 8 ounces each

> *Beurre Blanc*
> ½ cup plus 3 tablespoons butter
> ½ medium cucumber, peeled, halved,
>   and sliced
> ½ cup dry white wine
> 1 tablespoon minced shallots
> Lime juice, to taste
> Coarsely chopped cilantro, to taste
> Salt and pepper, to taste

1. Combine the oil, chiles, chopped cilantro, and salt and marinate the chicken or fish in this mixture for ½ hour.

2. Grill the chicken or fish until barely done.

3. While the chicken cooks, melt 3 tablespoons of the butter in a skillet and cook the cucumber until softened, about 3 minutes. Meanwhile, boil the wine and shallots together in a small saucepan until reduced to 1 tablespoon. Remove the saucepan from the heat and add the remaining butter to the saucepan bit by bit, whisking constantly. Add the softened cucumbers and season to taste with lime juice, cilantro, salt, and pepper. Serve over the chicken or fish.

Note: With a little practice, you should be able to make the sauce in the time it takes the chicken or fish to cook. If you start the sauce ahead of time, keep it warm in a water bath, or reheat it very gently if at all.

CHICKEN BREASTS
WITH ROASTED GARLIC-GOAT CHEESE SAUCE

I first ate roasted garlic in Italy, and my life has never been the same since. A roasted head of garlic can be combined with a multitude of things, each one tasting better than the next. It goes wonderfully with cheese, not just the goat cheese here but also Brie and other varieties. This sauce is just as good with pasta as it is over chicken breasts.

As long as you are roasting one head of garlic for this dish, you might want to roast several more. They have many uses, including the sauce for the Sonoran Shrimp Cocktail on page 60, and will keep for a week in the refrigerator.

Serves 6

    1 whole head garlic
    1 tablespoon olive oil
    3 cups cream
    2 tablespoons butter
    4 ounces goat cheese
    Salt and white pepper, to taste
    6 whole boned chicken breasts,
        skin on or skinless as you prefer

1. Brush the whole garlic head with olive oil, wrap it in foil, and bake for 2 hours in a 200°F oven. Meanwhile, bring the cream to a simmer and reduce by half.

2. Let the roasted garlic cool enough to handle. Melt the butter in a skillet. Cut off the top of the garlic and squeeze the soft cloves out into the skillet. Cook slowly, stirring, until the garlic combines with the butter into a smooth paste. Add the reduced cream and goat cheese and simmer until smooth. Season with salt and white pepper.

3. Grill, bake, or saute the chicken breasts until they just spring back when pressed with a fingertip. Serve with the garlic sauce.

GRILLED CHICKEN
WITH CALABACITAS

~~~~~~~~~~

Calabacitas literally means squash, particularly zucchini and other summer squashes; but when it appears on a menu it means a concoction that includes much more than just squash. It's delicious as a side dish for any grilled or roasted fowl or meat.

Any chicken can be used in this recipe, but free-range chickens are the most flavorful.

Serves 6

2 free-range chickens, 3½ pounds each, quartered or cut up
¼ cup olive oil
2 teaspoons chopped garlic
2 teaspoons chile powder

Calabacitas
4 tablespoons olive oil
1 medium white onion, diced
1 tablespoon chopped garlic
3 yellow squash, diced
3 zucchini or other green summer squash, diced
1 cup corn kernels, fresh or frozen
1 small red bell pepper, roasted, peeled, and seeded (see page 24) and cut into strips
1 small green bell pepper, roasted, peeled, and seeded and cut into strips
¼ cup white wine
½ cup cream
2 tablespoons chopped fresh marjoram
Salt and pepper, to taste
2 tablespoons *each* Monterey jack and cheddar cheeses

Tomato-Pepper Relish
3 red bell peppers, seeded and chopped
2 small tomatoes, chopped
1 bunch cilantro, coarsely chopped
1 tablespoon chopped garlic
1 tablespoon olive oil
Juice of ½ lime
Salt and pepper, to taste

1. Rub the chicken with the oil and garlic and sprinkle with chile powder. Grill over a medium-hot fire or bake until the juices run clear.

2. For the calabacitas, heat the oil in a large skillet and saute the onion and garlic until soft. Add the squash, corn, and peppers and saute lightly. Add the wine, stirring to deglaze the bottom of the pan, and simmer until the vegetables are just tender. Add the cream, marjoram, salt, and pepper and cook until the cream is slightly reduced. Add cheese to thicken. If the calabacitas is ready before the chicken, keep it warm, or reheat gently at serving time.

3. Combine the Tomato-Pepper Relish ingredients and mix well.

4. Divide the calabacitas among the plates and serve the grilled chicken on top. Garnish with the relish.

CHICKEN BREAST SANDWICH
WITH MELTED JARLSBERG

This is the "Big Mac" of Café Terra Cotta. We have thought often that we should have some type of golden arches to announce the number we have sold over the years. We grill the chicken breasts because we always have the grill going in the restaurant and because grilling gives them the best flavor; but you can cook them under the broiler or even in a saute pan if that is more convenient.

Serves 8

  ½ cup mayonnaise
  1 cup Salsa Fresca (page 37)
  8 whole chicken breasts (8 ounces each),
      skinned and boned
  8 slices country bread, ½ inch thick,
      lightly toasted
  16 thin slices Jarlsberg cheese

1. Combine the mayonnaise and ½ cup of the salsa. Let stand 1 hour in the refrigerator for the flavors to combine.

2. Grill, broil, or saute the chicken breasts. Spread the bread with the salsa mayonnaise. Place the chicken breasts on the bread, top with cheese, and melt under the broiler.

3. Serve open-face with shoestring potatoes and a dollop of salsa fresca.

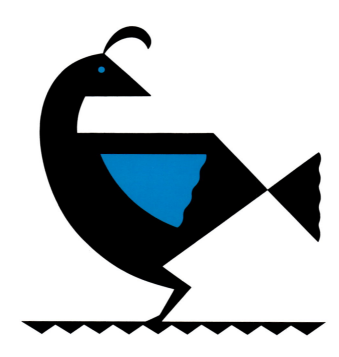

QUAIL IN ESCABECHE
WITH MOLE VERDE

〰〰〰〰〰

Quail offers an alternative to eating chicken so often, and because it cooks quickly it is very convenient. Both the marinade and the sauce can be made a day ahead, so the whole dish comes together quickly and easily. Corn and Pepper Spoonbread (page 131) makes a good side dish, or if you have some left over, a good stuffing for the quail.

Serves 6

Escabeche
2 teaspoons black peppercorns
½ teaspoon ground allspice
½ teaspoon ground cloves
½ teaspoon cumin seeds
4 teaspoons oregano leaves
4 tablespoons roasted garlic
1 teaspoon salt
2 tablespoons cider vinegar
2 teaspoons flour

〰〰〰

12 quail, trimmed of any excess skin and fat

Mole Verde
1 cup pumpkin seeds
3 cups Basic Chicken Stock (page 20)
8 tomatillos, husked and washed
2 jalapeño OR 4 serrano chiles
5 romaine lettuce leaves
½ medium onion, coarsely chopped
1 teaspoon chopped garlic
6 sprigs cilantro
⅛ teaspoon ground cumin
Pinch of black pepper
1 teaspoon ground cinnamon
Pinch of ground cloves
2 tablespoons olive oil
Salt and pepper, to taste

1. For the Escabeche: Grind the spices together in a spice grinder. Transfer to a bowl and add the garlic and salt. Work into a smooth paste. Work in the vinegar and flour and rub a thin layer on the quail, inside and out. Marinate several hours or overnight in the refrigerator.

2. For the Mole Verde: Toast the pumpkin seeds in a skillet until all have toasted and popped. Let cool completely, then grind in a spice grinder. Transfer to a small bowl and stir in 1 cup of the chicken broth. Set aside.

3. Simmer the tomatillos and chiles in water until soft, 10 to 15 minutes. Drain and place in a blender with the lettuce, onion, garlic, cilantro, and spices. Process until smooth.

4. Heat the oil in a saucepan over medium heat. Add the pumpkin seed mixture and stir constantly as it thickens and darkens, 4 to 5 minutes. Add the tomatillo puree. Cook and stir until very thick. Stir in the remaining 2 cups of stock, reduce the heat, and simmer for 30 minutes. Use a little more stock if necessary to reach a medium-thick consistency. Adjust the seasoning with salt and pepper.

5. Grill the quail over a moderate fire or bake at 375°F until the juices from the thigh run clear when pierced with a fork, approximately 20 minutes. Spoon the mole verde onto warm plates and serve the quail on top.

GRILLED DUCK BREAST
WITH MOLE SAUCE AND MANGO SALSA

Mole has gotten a rather strange reputation as a "chocolate sauce" for poultry. Chocolate duck is certainly not my cup of tea either; but there is much more to a good mole than just chocolate. It's only one of a long list of ingredients, and it's certainly not the predominant flavor. It merely adds another element to a complex mixture of chile, spices, nuts, and dried fruits. The long list of ingredients in most mole recipes scares away some cooks, but this one is extremely manageable, and it has some surprise ingredients. It was developed by Steve Critcher, one of our chefs in Tucson from 1988 to 1994.

For more on the fascinating subject of moles, I recommend the books by Patricia Quintana, Diana Kennedy, and Rick and Deann Bayless.

Serves 6

½ pound (approximately 15 to 18)
    dried ancho chiles
2 tablespoons olive oil
1 onion, chopped
2 tablespoons water
⅓ cup walnuts, chopped
1 ripe banana
⅓ cup raisins
1½ ounces crystallized ginger
⅔ cup orange juice
3 tablespoons tequila
1½ tablespoons roasted garlic
    (see Chicken Breasts with Roasted
    Garlic and Goat Cheese Sauce, page 111)

⅓ tablespoon ground espresso
1 teaspoon ground cumin
⅓ teaspoon ground coriander
2 teaspoons ground cinnamon
⅓ teaspoon ground cloves
1 teaspoon chipotle chile
3 tablespoons Coca-Cola (really!)
2 ounces bittersweet chocolate
Salt, to taste

Mango Salsa
2 ripe mangoes
1 red bell pepper, seeded and diced
1 yellow bell pepper, seeded and diced
1 poblano chile, seeded and diced
1 jalapeño chile, seeded and diced
1 bunch cilantro, leaves only, finely chopped
1/4 cup lime juice
Salt and pepper, to taste

6 duck breasts, trimmed and skin scored

1. Toast the ancho chiles on a cookie sheet in a 450°F oven (or on a dry skillet or griddle, if you don't have the oven on) for 2 minutes, or until fragrant and pliable. Remove the stems and seeds and soak the chiles overnight in water to remove bitterness.

2. Drain the chiles and discard the soaking liquid. Heat the olive oil in a skillet and saute the onion until soft. Add the soaked and drained chiles and saute 5 minutes. Add fresh water to cover and simmer 30 minutes.

3. Lift the chiles and onion out of the pan with a slotted spoon and transfer them to a food processor or blender. Puree, adding a little of the cooking liquid if necessary. Add the walnuts, banana, raisins, ginger, orange juice, and tequila. Puree until smooth. Add the garlic, espresso, cumin, coriander, cinnamon, cloves, and chipotle. Puree again.

4. Transfer the mixture to a saucepan and simmer 30 minutes. Remove from the heat and stir in the Coca-Cola and chocolate. Season with salt to taste.

5. While the sauce simmers, prepare the salsa: Cut the mango flesh from the pits. Remove the skin and cut the flesh into small cubes. Add the peppers, chile, and cilantro and mix well. Add the lime juice and season to taste with salt and pepper.

6. Grill or broil the duck breasts until medium rare. Slice crosswise and set aside. Place some mole on each plate and fan a duck breast across it. Top with mango salsa. Serve with Savory Black Beans (page 133) or Arroz Verde (below), and flour tortillas for guests to roll their own tacos.

ARROZ VERDE
(GREEN RICE)

This is an excellent accompaniment to many of the main course dishes in this cookbook. Plain white rice will never satisfy after you have tasted green rice.

Serves 6

2 large poblano chiles, roasted and peeled
    (see page 24)
½ bunch cilantro, washed, dried,
    and chopped
2 cloves garlic
2 serrano chiles, chopped with seeds
2 cups water or chicken stock
1½ tablespoons butter
½ teaspoon salt
2 tablespoons corn oil
1 small onion, diced
¾ cup white rice

1. Blend the poblanos, cilantro, garlic, and serranos in a food processor or blender. Combine with the water or stock, butter, and salt in a large saucepan. Bring to a soft boil.

2. Heat the oil in a skillet and saute the onion and rice until golden brown. Add to the pan of flavored stock and stir thoroughly. Cover and simmer until the rice is tender and has absorbed all the liquid.

BAKED STUFFED POBLANO CHILES

As I noted in the appetizers chapter, *chiles rellenos* simply means "stuffed chiles." Any large pepper can be stuffed, but I much prefer the poblano chile for its flavor, although when they run hot, they can be very hot! The plain cheese stuffing in the typical north-of-the-border version also gives no hint of the possibilities in authentic Mexican stuffings, which often include raisins, nuts, and other ingredients to add flavor and texture. Here are two examples. You could also use the stuffing for the Three-Cheese Chiles Rellenos on page 48.

Serves 4

> 8 nicely shaped poblano chiles
>
> *Raisin Stuffing*
> 2 medium onions, chopped and sauteed in butter until soft
> 2 cups shredded Monterey jack cheese
> 2 cups raisins
> 1 jalapeño chile, finely chopped (optional)

> 1 cup shredded Monterey jack cheese
> 1 cup Salsa Fresca (page 37)

1. Roast and peel the chiles as directed on page 24. Make a slit in the side of each chile and remove the seeds, but not the stems. Combine the stuffing ingredients thoroughly and stuff evenly into the chiles.

2. Preheat the oven to 350°F. Place the stuffed chiles in an ungreased baking dish, add a little water in the bottom of the dish, and bake for 30 minutes.

3. Top the rellenos with the remaining shredded cheese and return them to the oven to melt the cheese (or if you prefer, run them under the broiler until the cheese is lightly browned. Serve with a dollop of salsa.

Variation:

CHICKEN-CORN STUFFING

> 2 medium onions, chopped and sauteed in butter until soft
> 2 whole chicken breasts, lightly grilled, cut in small cubes
> 2 cups Monterey jack cheese, grated
> 2 cups cut corn
> 1 jalapeño chile, finely chopped (optional)

Combine the ingredients and use in place of the raisin stuffing above.

SOUTHWESTERN MEAT LOAF
WITH YUCATECAN RED CHILE SAUCE

This original Café Terra Cotta recipe has not been on the menu for years, but I would not hesitate to bring it back. With today's emphasis on "back to basics" this should be very popular.

Serves 8

2 ounces whole dried pasilla chiles
  (*chile negro*) (see page 18)
2 ounces whole dried New Mexico chiles
  (dried "red" chiles)

Meat Loaf
2 pounds ground beef
3 eggs, lightly beaten
1 cup finely chopped onion
2 tablespoons minced garlic
1 teaspoon ground California or
  New Mexico chile
3 Anaheim chiles, roasted, peeled,
  and finely chopped
½ cup Salsa Fresca (page 37)
Salt and pepper, to taste

2 large garlic cloves
2 tablespoons *each* orange and lemon juice
¼ teaspoon *each* orange and lemon zest
¾ teaspoon ground cumin
¼ teaspoon cayenne pepper
¾ teaspoon paprika
¼ teaspoon oregano
2 tablespoons olive oil
1 tablespoon white wine
1 tablespoon butter
Salt and pepper, to taste

1. Slit the chiles open, remove the seeds, and place the chiles in a bowl. Pour boiling water over the chiles and soak for one hour.

2. Preheat the oven to 350°F. Mix the meat loaf ingredients together thoroughly and bake in a loaf pan to an internal temperature of 165°F, about 1 hour.

3. While the meat loaf bakes, prepare the sauce: Drain the soaked chiles and reserve the soaking liquid. Chop the garlic in a food processor. Add the drained chiles, citrus juices and zest, and spices. Puree to a paste. Add the olive oil and thin with reserved soaking liquid until smooth. Strain the sauce into a saucepan, add the wine and butter, and simmer until well blended, about 15 minutes. Season with salt and pepper and keep warm.

4. Slice the meat loaf and serve in a pool of the chile sauce.

Variation: This sauce is a perfect way to explore the subtle differences in flavor among the various dried chiles. The particular combination of pasilla and New Mexico chiles is a personal favorite, but try it with whatever large dried chiles you can find — ancho, cascabel, guajillo, whatever your local markets carry.

GRILLED FILET MIGNON
WITH RED CHILE CREAM SAUCE

The traditional French way to serve filet mignon is with Béarnaise sauce. The creamy richness of the butter and egg yolk sauce enhances the very tender beef, but the key to the balance is the slight bite from the vinegar-wine reduction. This sauce works in the same way, with ancho chile providing a bite which is softened by the cream. This sauce goes well with other tender cuts of beef such as sliced châteaubriand or sirloin tips, and is also delicious with pork or chicken.

Serves 4

    3 dried ancho chiles
    2 cups cream
    1 cup dry white wine
    3 garlic cloves, roasted (see page 111)
        and pureed
    Pinch of cayenne
    Salt and pepper, to taste
    8 filet mignon medallions, 3 ounces each

1. Slit open the chiles and remove the stems and seeds. Soak the chiles in boiling water to cover for 30 minutes. Remove from the bowl, puree in a blender with a little of the soaking liquid, and set aside.

2. Combine the cream, wine, and garlic in a saucepan and reduce by half. Add the chile puree and seasonings and mix thoroughly.

3. Grill or broil the medallions to the desired doneness. Spread the sauce on warm plates and serve the medallions on top.

Note: The sauce can be made up to 2 days ahead of time and refrigerated. Reheat gently before serving.

Variation: Like the sauce for the meat loaf on page 120, this sauce can be made with other chile varities such as cascabel, guajillo, or pasilla, perhaps with a small amount of chipotle included with another variety.

GRILLED RIB EYE STEAK
WITH SOUTHWESTERN BARBECUE SAUCE

Never can a bottled barbecue sauce taste as good as a freshly made one. My usual complaint with barbecue sauces is that they are too sweet. This one hits the perfect balance between sweet and savory. It's also good on other meats and poultry.

Serves 6

Sauce
8 large ripe tomatoes, peeled, seeded, and chopped
1 onion, chopped
¼ cup molasses
2 tablespoons balsamic vinegar
2 tablespoons cider vinegar
2 tablespoons orange juice
½ cup red wine
2 teaspoons Worcestershire sauce
1 teaspoon *each* ground allspice, cloves, and black pepper
¼ teaspoon Dijon mustard
¼ teaspoon cumin
½ teaspoon ground coriander
¼ teaspoon paprika
¼ teaspoon ground ginger
2 cloves garlic, minced
1 dried ancho chile, stem and seeds removed

6 rib eye steaks, 8 ounces each (preferably Certified Angus — see page 100)

1. Combine all the sauce ingredients in a large pot. Bring to a boil, reduce the heat, and simmer until all the ingredients are blended and the sauce begins to thicken, about 20 minutes. Remove from the heat and puree (in batches if necessary) in a blender or food processor.

2. Brush the steaks very, very lightly with the sauce and grill or broil them to the desired degree of doneness. Warm the remaining sauce and serve on the side. We serve this dish with the onion rings on page 133.

LAMB CHOPS
WITH DRIED CHERRY-CHIPOTLE SAUCE

Marianne Banes, our chef in Tucson from 1989 to 1994, was quick to jump on sun-dried cherries when they became available to us. They offer a wonderful texture to the sauce, and in combination with the chipotle chiles, a great depth of flavor as well. Be sure to use the tart variety, made from bright red Montmorency cherries, rather than the sweet, black Bing type. Wild Rice Pancakes (recipe follows) are an ideal side dish for this or the other lamb chop recipe on page 126.

Serves 4

 1½ cups sun-dried cherries
 1 small red onion, finely chopped
 1 tablespoon chopped garlic
 1 tablespoon oil
 1 cup Basic Chicken Stock (page 20)
 ¼ cup dry red wine
 2 tablespoons crème de cassis or brandy
 1 tablespoon chopped chipotle chiles
 Salt and pepper, to taste
 12 to 16 rib or loin lamb chops

1. Soak the cherries in water to cover overnight, or for at least 1 hour. Do not drain.

2. Saute the onion and garlic in oil until slightly caramelized. Add the cherries and their soaking liquid, stock, wine, and crème de cassis or brandy. Simmer until the liquid is reduced by a quarter. Let cool slightly and add the chipotles. Puree and season to taste.

3. Grill or broil the lamb chops to the desired doneness. Reheat the sauce gently, thinning it with water if necessary. Spoon onto warm plates and serve the chops on top.

Note: The sauce can be made up to 2 days ahead of time and refrigerated. It also goes well with pork, beef, or chicken.

WILD RICE PANCAKES

Even though wild rice is not native to the Southwest, its crunchy texture and nutty flavor seem right at home in contemporary southwestern cuisine. These cakes can accompany almost any of the meat or poultry entrees in this chapter.

Makes 16 4-inch or 20 3-inch pancakes
(8 servings)

½ pound wild rice, cooked (1¼ cups)
2 stalks celery, diced
4 green onions, sliced thinly
1 teaspoon garlic, minced
¼ teaspoon cayenne
Pinch of chile powder
2 teaspoons salt, or to taste
¼ teaspoon pepper, or to taste
4 eggs, lightly beaten
⅓ to ½ cup flour
4 tablespoons oil

1. Mix the wild rice, celery, onions, garlic, and spices. Season to taste with salt and pepper. Stir in the eggs, then enough flour to bind the mixture; the texture should be firm but still moist, not glued together.

2. To cook, heat a small amount of oil in a skillet over medium heat. Form the cakes by spooning the batter into the pan and flattening it gently with the back of the spoon. Cook until crisp, 2 to 3 minutes per side.

LAMB CHOPS
WITH TEQUILA AND HONEY

This is an easy dish to prepare once you have made some veal stock (or even lamb stock). If you have neither, you can use reduced chicken stock, though the flavor won't be quite the same. The tequila adds an edge that balances the sweetness and syrupy consistency of the sauce.

Serves 3 to 4

> ½ cup olive oil
> Juice of 1½ limes (about 3 tablespoons)
> Pinch of ground cumin
> Pinch of cayenne
> Pinch of chile powder
> 12 rib lamb chops (3 to 4 pounds in all)
> 2 cups reduced veal stock (see page 20)
> ¼ cup honey
> ¼ cup tequila
> 4 tablespoons butter
> Salt and pepper, to taste
> Lime peel, cut into fine julienne

1. Combine the olive oil, juice of 1 lime, cumin, cayenne, and chile powder. Marinate the lamb chops in this mixture for at least 4 hours.

2. While the lamb is marinating, cook the veal stock and remaining lime juice together until it starts to reduce and thicken, about 10 minutes. Add the honey and simmer 5 minutes. Add the tequila and simmer 1 minute to cook off some of the alcohol. Just before serving, stir in the butter and correct the seasoning with salt and pepper.

3. Grill or broil the lamb chops to the desired doneness. Spoon the tequila sauce over the chops and garnish with lime peel.

Variation:

LAMB CHOPS WITH PRICKLY PEAR GLAZE

Add ½ cup prickly pear syrup and 1 tablespoon apricot puree to the sauce in place of the honey and reduce until thickened.

Note: Other lamb chops, including loin (sometimes called diamond cut) and shoulder chops, may be substituted for the rib chops.

SMOKED PORK LOIN
WITH WHITE BEAN CHILI

Pork dishes are generally difficult to sell in restaurants. This recipe was one of the original recipes when Café Terra Cotta opened and even though it has been off the menu for many years, it remains one of my favorites. Note that the chili can be made entirely ahead of time and reheated, or it can simmer while the pork loin cooks. Start the chili ahead of time if using tenderloins, which will cook in less than 30 minutes in the smoker.

Serves 6 to 8

    1 pound dried Great Northern beans
    1 tablespoon butter
    1 medium onion, finely chopped
    1 carrot, peeled and chopped
    2 celery stalks, chopped
    2 tablespoons pure ground chile
        (California or New Mexico)
    1½ teaspoons ground cumin
    ¼ teaspoon cayenne
    2 cloves garlic, chopped
    2 teaspoons salt
    ¾ teaspoon freshly ground pepper
    6 cups (approximately) chicken stock
    3 pounds boneless pork loin roast
    1½ to 2 cups Salsa Fresca (page 37)

1. Soak the dried beans in cold water to cover overnight. (If in a hurry, see page 25 for a quick soak process.)

2. Melt the butter in a heavy saucepan over medium heat. Mix in the onion, carrot, and celery. Cover and cook, stirring occasionally, until the vegetables are tender. Add the chile powder, cumin, cayenne, garlic, salt, and pepper. Cook 2 minutes.

3. Drain the beans and add them to the pot with enough chicken stock to cover by 2 inches. Bring to a boil, skimming the surface as necessary. Reduce the heat, cover partially, and simmer until the beans are tender but not mushy, about 1½ hours.

4. While the beans simmer, set up a wok for smoking (see page 23). Place the pork loin on the rack and smoke for 30 minutes. Transfer to a roasting pan and roast in a 375°F oven to an internal temperature of 150°F, about 1 hour.

5. Serve the beans in a soup bowl with sliced pork on top. Garnish with Salsa Fresca.

Note: How much to cook pork is a matter of personal preference. I like it cooked to an internal temperature of 150°F, when it is still slightly pink inside; feel free to cook it more if you prefer.

PORK TENDERLOIN
WITH APRICOT CHUTNEY

In hot climates, dried fruit offers a way to use fruits when the fresh versions are out of season or not plentiful. Drying also intensifies their flavor, and the concentrated flavor of dried apricots is especially complimentary to pork. Pork tenderloin has gained tremendous popularity in the last few years; it's low in fat and low in price for such a tender cut of meat. Once hard to find, whole boneless tenderloins are readily available in supermarkets.

Serves 6

   1½ cup dried apricot halves
   1 cup raisins
   3 cups water
   1½ teaspoons grated orange zest
   1½ teaspoons grated lime zest
   2 jalapeño chiles, finely chopped
      (remove the seeds if desired)
   2 medium red bell peppers, seeded
      and chopped
   1 cup orange juice, preferably fresh
   2 tablespoons fresh lime juice
   2½ cups sugar
   6 whole pork tenderloins

1. Soak the apricots and raisins in water for several hours or overnight.

2. Pour the dried fruits with their soaking water into a saute pan, adding more liquid to at least half the depth of the fruit. Add the zests, jalapeños, and bell peppers and simmer for about 15 minutes or until tender.

3. Add the juices and bring to a boil. Reduce the heat, add the sugar, and simmer, stirring very frequently, until the liquid has almost evaporated, about 30 minutes. Let cool before serving.

4. Grill the tenderloins over a medium-hot fire, or roast in a 450°F oven, or smoke in a wok (see page 23); total cooking time will be 20 to 30 minutes, depending on the method and the intensity of the heat. Use a meat thermometer to test for doneness (see Note, page 127). Slice and arrange decoratively on warm plates. Spoon chutney over the slices.

Note: The chutney can be made up to 3 days ahead of time and refrigerated. Serve slightly warmed or at room temperature.

Variation: For additional flavor, marinate the pork tenderloins in *adobado*, a seasoning paste that is equally good on pork, chicken, or fish. Combine 1 cup brown sugar, ¼ cup chile powder, 2 tablespoons lime juice, ¼ teaspoon each salt and pepper, 2 teaspoons minced garlic, and 1 teaspoon olive oil and mix to a paste. Rub the paste on the meat and marinate anywhere from ½ hour to overnight in the refrigerator. Grill, roast, or smoke as above. *Adobado* is not to be confused with *adobo*, the vinegar-based sauce used for pickling or as a marinade for grilled foods (see Scallops in Adobo, page 105).

PENNE WITH THREE CHEESES

This recipe is one of our most popular pasta dishes. We use mesquite-smoked bacon because of its southwestern orientation and for its distinctive, robust flavor. If mesquite-smoked bacon is unavailable, use any thickly sliced, flavorful bacon. Or the bacon can be left out to make a vegetarian dish.

Serves 4 as an entree, 6 as a side dish or first course

8 ounces ricotta cheese
1 cup cream or half-and-half
1 teaspoon chopped garlic
1 medium tomato, coarsely chopped
¼ cup chopped cilantro
4 slices thick sliced bacon, well cooked, drained, and cut into ½-inch pieces

1 tablespoon hot pepper flakes OR
    4 chiletepíns, crumbled
1 cup grated mozzarella cheese
    (about 2½ ounces)
¼ cup grated Parmesan cheese
8 ounces penne pasta, cooked and drained
¼ cup chopped parsley, for garnish

1. Beat the ricotta, cream, and garlic together. Place in a skillet with the tomato, cilantro, bacon, and pepper flakes. Warm over medium heat, then add the mozzarella and 2 to 3 tablespoons of the Parmesan. Heat over low heat until the mozzarella is melted.

2. Add the cooked and drained penne to the skillet and heat gently, mixing carefully. Serve in wide soup bowls. Garnish with parsley and the reserved Parmesan.

CORN AND PEPPER
SPOONBREAD

Spoonbread is a southern dish that may have been borrowed from Italy because it starts out like polenta. We have turned it southwestern by the addition of sweet corn kernels, red bell peppers, and a touch of chile.

Serves 8

2½ cups water
2 teaspoons salt
4 tablespoons butter
Pinch of white pepper
1 cup fine yellow cornmeal
1 cup buttermilk
5 eggs
⅓ cup cream
1 cup corn kernels
1 cup diced red bell peppers
½ teaspoon crushed chiltepín
Chopped cilantro, for garnish

1. Bring the water, salt, butter, and white pepper to a simmer. Slowly add the cornmeal and continue to simmer, stirring, until it is very thick and coats the bottom of the pan, about 5 minutes.

2. Preheat the oven to 400°F. Beat in the remaining ingredients and pour into a greased 9x12-inch baking dish. Bake until set and browned, 30 to 45 minutes. Garnish each serving with chopped cilantro.

Note: Any leftovers can be cooled and used as a stuffing for quail, chicken, or pork.

Onion Rings
with Seasoned Flour

We serve these with the barbecue steak on page 123, but they are good with any grilled or roast meat.

Serves 6

Oil for deep-frying
2 cups all-purpose flour
2 tablespoons paprika
½ teaspoon salt
½ teaspoon cayenne

¼ teaspoon curry powder
3 large onions, sliced very thin
    and separated into rings
1 cup buttermilk

Heat oil for deep-frying to 375°F. Combine the flour and seasonings. Toss the onion slices in the buttermilk, dip in the seasoned flour, and fry in batches until golden brown, about 3 minutes. Drain and serve immediately.

Savory Black Beans

I adore black beans and take my guidance on this recipe from my long-time friend Marge Poore, who teaches Mexican cooking in the San Francisco Bay Area.

Serves 6 to 8

1 pound dry black beans
2 bay leaves
½ teaspoon crumbled oregano
½ medium onion, chopped
1 sprig epazote, if available
2 tablespoons vegetable oil
Salt and pepper, to taste

1. Check the beans for any pebbles. Rinse thoroughly and soak overnight or use the quick soak process on page 25.

2. Drain the beans and put them into a large pot with the bay leaves and oregano. Add water to cover by 2 inches. Bring to a boil, reduce the heat, cover, and simmer until just soft, approximately 1 hour. Add the onion, epazote, and oil and simmer another 30 to 40 minutes. Season to taste with salt and pepper and cook another 10 minutes or so.

Note: Other herbs and spices may be added to black beans; see the Black Bean Chili recipe on page 77 for ideas.

Black beans will keep in the refrigerator for up to 5 days, but after they sit for a day or two they may need to be resalted. Check the seasoning and correct if necessary before serving.

DESSERTS

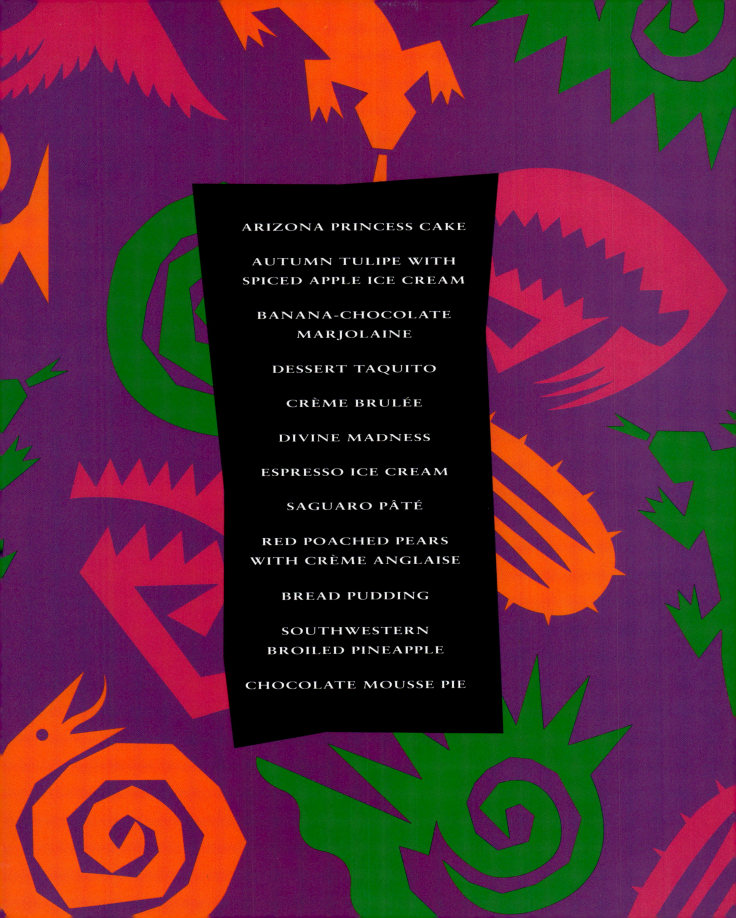

ARIZONA PRINCESS CAKE

AUTUMN TULIPE WITH
SPICED APPLE ICE CREAM

BANANA-CHOCOLATE
MARJOLAINE

DESSERT TAQUITO

CRÈME BRULÉE

DIVINE MADNESS

ESPRESSO ICE CREAM

SAGUARO PÂTÉ

RED POACHED PEARS
WITH CRÈME ANGLAISE

BREAD PUDDING

SOUTHWESTERN
BROILED PINEAPPLE

CHOCOLATE MOUSSE PIE

When it comes to desserts, I admit it — I am one of those people who think about dessert before I start composing or ordering a meal. (I subscribe to the motto "life is short, order dessert first.") And after the robust flavors of a southwestern meal, dessert time is no time to back away from flavorful food. The stage has been set, and your palate is ready for something equally memorable for dessert.

In desserts more than anywhere else on the menu, "contemporary southwestern" becomes a matter of personal interpretation. Unlike other regions such as New England and the Deep South, the Southwest has not contributed any famous desserts to American regional cuisine. Many authentic Mexican desserts are not particularly suited to American tastes; they tend to be overly sweet, and they sometimes use fruits like maguey and sapote that are very difficult to obtain in the U.S.

This absence of tradition allows me the maximum freedom to improvise and create desserts that complement contemporary southwestern cuisine, even to play around with such items as dessert *taquitos* (see page 143). The desserts here and on the menu at Café Terra Cotta are mostly based in my classic French training. And, as I am a "chocoholic," I lean heavily toward anything chocolate.

In this chapter are some of my favorites from our dessert menu. For those who are not so crazy about chocolate, I have included a few based on fruit. All of them reflect the basic value that runs throughout our menu and this book — flavorful. I hope they provide you with the perfect ending to many an unforgettable meal.

ARIZONA PRINCESS CAKE

This dense, rich cake combines Arizona apples and pecans with a generous splash of tequila. My thanks to Alice Medrich for her inspiration.

Serves 12

⅓ cup dried apples, minced
⅓ cup tequila
8 ounces bittersweet chocolate, chopped
½ cup (4 ounces) butter
3 large eggs, separated
⅔ cup granulated sugar
¼ cup all-purpose flour
⅔ cup finely chopped toasted pecans
    (see Note)

Glaze
½ cup (4 ounces) butter
8 ounces bittersweet chocolate, chopped
1 tablespoon corn syrup

½ cup chopped toasted pecans (optional)
12 pecan halves, toasted

1. Steep the dried apples in tequila for ½ hour. Grease an 8-inch round cake pan and line the bottom with a circle of parchment. Flour the pan and tap out any excess.

2. Preheat the oven to 375°F. Combine the chocolate and butter in the top of a double boiler and melt over hot water. Remove from the heat and set aside.

3. Beat the egg yolks with half the sugar until pale yellow. Stir in the chocolate mixture, flour, and the ⅔ cup chopped pecans until thoroughly blended. Add the apples and tequila.

4. In another bowl, beat the egg whites to the soft peak stage, then add the remaining sugar. Continue beating until firm. Gently stir a third of the beaten egg whites into the batter to lighten it, then fold in the remaining egg whites. Pour the batter into the prepared pan and bake until a toothpick inserted in the middle comes out slightly moist, about 40 minutes. The cake should remain slightly moist in the center. Let the cake cool in the pan on a rack. Press down the edges to make them level with the center, which sinks slightly as it cools. Turn out onto a cardboard round or directly onto the rack, bottom side up.

5. Combine the glaze ingredients in a double boiler and melt over warm water. Stir until smooth. Remove from the heat and let cool to a spreading consistency. Spread a thin "crumb coating" of glaze over the top and sides of the cake and chill for 10 minutes.

6. Reheat the remaining glaze over hot water until smooth, but not too hot. Place the cake on a rack over a plate or cookie sheet. Pour all the glaze through a sieve onto the cake. Quickly spread the glaze over the edges of the cake with a spatula, letting it run down the sides. Let the glaze dry slightly, then coat the sides with the optional chopped toasted nuts. Decorate the top with 12 toasted pecan halves.

Note: To toast pecans, place shelled halves on a baking sheet in one layer and toast them in a 300°F oven until medium brown, watching carefully to make sure they don't burn. Cool. Save 12 halves for decoration. Chop the remaining pecans coarsely in a food processor. This step can be done while the apples are steeping.

AUTUMN TULIPE
WITH SPICED APPLE ICE CREAM

⌄⌄⌄⌄⌄⌄⌄

Tulipes, edible cups made from various thin cookies bent into holders, have become very standard on dessert menus. These *tulipes* can be used and named for spring, summer, or winter depending on how you fill them. Every fall I like to use apples in some way and this is my first choice after my mom's apple pie.

Serves 8 to 10

> 3 tablespoons soft butter
> ¾ cup light brown sugar
> 6 tablespoons light corn syrup
> ¾ cup all-purpose flour
> ¾ ounce ground almonds
> Pinch of salt
> 1 recipe Spiced Apple Ice Cream
>   (page 140)
> ½ recipe Caramel Sauce (page 143)

1. Preheat the oven to 350°F. Mix the butter, brown sugar, and corn syrup together until smooth. Add the flour, ground almonds, and salt. Mix just until incorporated. Do not over-mix or the flour will become glutinous and the cookies will come out hard instead of tender-crisp.

2. Roll the cookie dough into balls about the size of large walnuts. Place 3 balls evenly spaced on a greased or sprayed cookie sheet. Bake until golden brown and covered with bubbles, 5 to 8 minutes, checking to be sure they don't burn around the edges. Cool slightly. While the cookies are still soft and flexible, lift them off the pan with a spatula and drape each one over the bottom of a small cup or juice glass. Repeat with the remaining balls of dough. (The *tulipes* should cool enough to hold their shape after a minute or so, so you should be able to make all the cups with two pans and one set of cups for molding.) Let the *tulipes* cool completely and store in an airtight container. If kept away from humidity, they should last for a week.

3. Fill the *tulipes* with spiced apple ice cream or any flavored ice cream that suits the season. Drizzle with Caramel Sauce.

SPICED APPLE ICE CREAM

This recipe starts with an ice cream base which can be adapted to make almost any flavor of ice cream. In this book, I also use it for the espresso ice cream to accompany Divine Madness (page 145).

Makes 1 quart

Ice Cream Base
4 cups cream
4 egg yolks
¾ cup sugar

6 apples, granny smith or firm
    golden delicious
¼ cup water
1 tablespoon lemon juice
2 tablespoons sugar
½ teaspoon ground cloves
½ teaspoon ground nutmeg
½ teaspoon ground cinnamon
2 tablespoons crystallized ginger, chopped

1. Combine the ice cream base ingredients in a bowl and whisk until smooth. Pour into a heavy saucepan and cook over medium heat, stirring constantly, until the mixture reaches 180°, or coats the back of a spoon as for crème anglaise. Do not let it boil. Strain into a bowl and let cool completely, then chill 2 hours to overnight.

2. Peel and core the apples and chop coarsely by hand or in a food processor. Place in a saucepan with the remaining ingredients. Cook on low heat to the consistency of chunky applesauce. Let cool completely.

3. Combine the chilled ice cream base and applesauce. Pour into an ice cream maker and freeze according to the manufacturer's instructions. Transfer to a freezer storage container and store in the freezer until ready to serve.

BANANA-CHOCOLATE MARJOLAINE

One of my favorite flavors to team with chocolate is banana. This recipe is based on merging a classic version of Gâteau Marjolaine and a banana version I tasted at Printers Row in Chicago.

Serves 8 to 10

Cake
1 cup hazelnuts, toasted
1 cup blanched almonds, toasted
1 cup sugar
2 teaspoons all-purpose flour
6 egg whites (¾ cup)
Unsweetened cocoa, for dusting

Ganache
1 cup cream
8 ounces bittersweet chocolate
4 tablespoons unsalted butter

Buttercream
1 cup sugar
2 eggs
1½ cups unsalted butter (soft)
1½ cups banana puree (about 3 bananas)
¼ cup praline paste, or to taste (see Note)

1. Cake: Preheat the oven to 450°F. Line a half sheet pan (12 by 17 inches) with parchment and grease the sides of the pan and the top of the parchment. Grind the hazelnuts, almonds, sugar, and flour together in a processor until very fine. Beat the egg whites until stiff and fold them into the nut mixture. Spread the batter onto the lined pan and bake until evenly browned, about 6 to 8 minutes. Turn the cake out immediately onto another piece of parchment that has been dusted with cocoa. Let cool.

2. Ganache: Bring the cream to a boil and remove from the heat. Add the chocolate and stir until smooth. Whisk in the butter and cool to spreading consistency.

3. Buttercream: Put the sugar in a heavy saucepan with water to cover. Swirl the pan by the handle to mix. Place over high heat and let cook until it reaches 240°F on a candy thermometer, or when a spoonful forms a soft ball when dropped into ice water. Do not stir the syrup as it cooks or it may crystallize. Remove the pan from the heat. Beat the eggs until blended, then pour in the hot syrup and continue beating until cool and thickened. Add the butter and beat until fluffy and smooth. Add the banana puree and praline paste to taste.

4. Assembly: Cut the cake lengthwise into 4 equal rectangles. Spread two pieces with buttercream, one with a thick layer of ganache, and the remaining one with a thin layer of ganache. Stack as follows: one piece of cake with buttercream, then the one with the thick ganache layer, then the other piece with buttercream, and finally the piece with the thin layer of ganache. Spread the sides with a thin layer of ganache and dust the top with cocoa. Slice crosswise to serve.

Note: Praline paste is sold in professional baker's supply stores, and you might find it in a well-stocked delicatessen. To make your own, caramelize ½ cup sugar with ¼ cup water (see page 143). When the caramel is well browned, stir in 1 cup toasted hazelnuts. Pour the mixture out onto a cookie sheet to cool thoroughly. Break the mixture into pieces and grind to a paste in a food processor.

DESSERT TAQUITO

The lack of traditions in southwestern desserts allows us to be creative, innovative, even playful, as in this case. *Taquitos,* also known as *flautas,* are small snacks of corn tortillas rolled around a filling and fried crisp. In this dessert version, a soft cornmeal crêpe plays the part of the tortilla, and sliced bananas and caramel sauce make up the filling. The taquitos are served on a zingy raspberry sauce flavored with chipotle chile.

Serves 8

Crêpes
1 cup water
1 cup milk
5 eggs
1 cup all-purpose flour
1 cup yellow cornmeal
¼ cup melted butter
2 tablespoons chopped mint leaves
⅓ cup oil, for cooking

Raspberry Sauce
2 packages (10 ounces each) frozen
    raspberries, strained
1 cup raspberry jam, strained
2 teaspoons pureed chipotle chile

4 ripe bananas, cut into ¼-inch slices
1 recipe Caramel Sauce, below
Powdered sugar
1 cup toasted pecans, chopped
1 cup cream, whipped with
    2 tablespoons sugar
Mint sprigs

1. Combine the crêpe batter ingredients (except the oil) in a blender or large food processor and blend until the flour is well mixed. Chill overnight. Cook the crêpes in a lightly oiled 6-inch crêpe pan, using about ⅛ cup batter for each crêpe (16 crêpes in all).

2. Mix the strained raspberries, jam, and chipotle chile together to make the sauce. Spoon 2 tablespoons of sauce onto each plate.

3. Place a few pieces of banana in each crêpe and drizzle with the caramel sauce. Roll and place two on each plate. Sprinkle with powdered sugar and chopped pecans. Garnish with a dollop of whipped cream and a sprig of mint.

CARAMEL SAUCE

Makes 2 cups

2 cups granulated sugar
1 cup water
2 cups cream
Juice of ½ lemon

Combine the sugar and water in a heavy saucepan and bring to a boil. Continue boiling (do not stir) until very brown, about the color of cola. Remove the pan from the heat and pour in the cream slowly. It will bubble and sizzle. When the bubbling subsides, add the lemon juice and return the pan to low heat. Simmer, stirring occasionally, until all the caramel has melted into the cream, about 10 minutes. Keep warm in a water bath until ready to serve.

Note: Use a condiment squeeze bottle for easy drizzling or plate painting.

CRÈME BRULÉE

"Burnt cream" is the literal translation of the name of this dish. It can mean either a cooked custard put into a pastry shell, or one like the following, where the custard is baked in a ramekin and then caramelized. This is the most creamy version I know of. The vanilla bean is of utmost importance to the flavor, and the tiny black specks that it leaves in the custard usually sink to the bottom during baking. Although granulated sugar can be used for the caramelized topping, brown sugar has given me the best results.

Serves 8 to 10

> 4 cups cream
> 1 whole vanilla bean
> 8 egg yolks
> ¾ cup sugar
> 4 tablespoons brown sugar for
>   caramelizing tops

1. Preheat the oven to 350°F. Set 8 to 10 (4½-ounce) ramekins in a roasting pan.

2. Combine the cream and the vanilla bean in a saucepan over medium heat. Simmer long enough to extract the flavor from the vanilla bean, about 5 minutes.

3. Meanwhile, combine the yolks and sugar in a large bowl and whisk together until blended.

4. Pour in the hot cream, whisking all the time to avoid curdling. Strain the custard into a large measuring cup or pitcher. Skim off any surface bubbles. Rinse off the vanilla bean; it can be reserved and used a second time.

5. Pour the custard into the ramekins, filling them to the top. Pour warm water into the pan to reach halfway up the sides of the ramekins. Cover the pan loosely with foil and bake until barely set. (Actual baking time will vary depending on the oven temperature, the shape of the ramekins, the weight of your cookware, even the amount of water in the pan, so start checking at 50 minutes and every 5 minutes thereafter.) Remove from the water bath and chill.

6. Spread the tops of the custards with a small amount of brown sugar and touch with a hot salamander, or broil very close to a heat source until all the sugar melts into brown caramel. A small hand-held propane torch (found in hardware stores) is another way to caramelize the tops.

Variation: For a coffee crème brulée, add 2 tablespoons instant coffee to the hot cream mixture. For chocolate, add approximately 6 ounces melted bittersweet chocolate. Orange zest and cinnamon are other flavors to try.

Note: A salamander is a cast iron disk anchored to a long handle, used to brown the tops of various dishes. The disk is heated directly over a hot burner until extremely hot, then held just above or pressed against the top of the food to be browned.

DIVINE MADNESS

Bittersweet chocolate and hazelnuts are my favorite sweet combination. Add to that butter and cream and the mixture becomes something that is sinfully good. Around the time I was developing this flourless cake, Bette Midler came out with her album called "The Divine Miss M," and suddenly I knew I had the perfect title for this outrageously delicious dessert.

Serves 10 to 12

> 1 pound bittersweet chocolate, chopped
> ½ cup hazelnut praline paste
>   (see Note, page 141)
> ½ cup cream
> ¾ cup butter
> 6 eggs, separated
> ⅓ cup sugar
> ⅔ cup ground toasted hazelnuts
> Powdered sugar

1. Preheat the oven to 350°F. Grease and flour a 9-inch springform pan.

2. Melt the chocolate, praline paste, cream, and butter together in a double boiler over lightly simmering water. Remove from the heat.

3. In a large bowl or electric mixer, beat the egg whites until soft peaks form. Add the sugar and continue to beat to the stiff peak stage. Add the egg yolks and beat for two minutes.

4. Fold half of the chocolate mixture and half of the nuts into the beaten eggs. Repeat with the remaining chocolate and nuts. Pour into the prepared pan and bake until not quite set in the middle, about 45 minutes. Let cool in the pan.

5. Remove the cake from the pan and dust with powdered sugar. Serve at room temperature.

ESPRESSO ICE CREAM

This cake is delicious by itself, but it's even better with a scoop of espresso ice cream. Prepare the ice cream base as directed on page 140. When the base is thoroughly chilled, add 3 tablespoons instant coffee and 2 tablespoons ground espresso-roast coffee. Freeze in an ice cream maker according to the manufacturer's instructions.

SAGUARO PÂTÉ

This dessert is basically a huge truffle. Although the decoration is a desert scene, it can be changed to fit any season, with a Christmas tree, a Valentine heart, or other cookie-cutter shape in place of the saguaro cactus. The decoration is put onto the pâté slice after it is cut.

Serves 12 to 16

2½ cups cream
1½ pounds bittersweet chocolate, chopped
¼ cup amaretto liqueur
2 teaspoons vanilla
¾ cup (6 ounces) unsalted butter
1 cup sliced almonds, toasted
2 packages (7 ounces) almond paste
Yellow food coloring
Green food coloring
Powdered sugar, for dusting
Optional: Crème Anglaise (page 148),
    flavored with 2 tablespoons amaretto

1. Cut a piece of parchment paper wide enough to match the length of a standard loaf pan. Use the paper to line the bottom and long sides of the pan (the ends do not have to be covered).

2. Bring the cream to a boil. Remove from the heat and stir in the chocolate until it is completely melted. Add the amaretto, vanilla, and butter. Stir until smooth.

3. Place about ⅓ of the mixture in a separate bowl and add the toasted almonds. Spread this mixture in the bottom of the loaf pan. Chill until firm, about 30 minutes. Pour in the remaining chocolate mixture (if it has hardened, melt it gently over hot water) and chill overnight.

4. Color about 3½ ounces of the almond paste with a few drops of yellow food coloring. Form it into a long cylinder about 1 inch in diameter and chill. Cut into circles approximately ⅛ inch thick.

5. Color the remaining almond paste with green food coloring to the desired darkness. Roll out the green almond paste to about ⅛ inch thickness, using powdered sugar on the board to keep it from sticking. Use a cookie cutter to cut the cactus shapes, one for each serving.

6. To serve, unmold the pâté and cut it into serving pieces about ½ inch thick. Spread a little amaretto crème anglaise on each plate and lay the slices of pâté on top. Place a cactus on each slice as if growing out the sand (the almond layer). Place the yellow moon (or sun) above it and slightly to the left.

Variation: Replace the crème anglaise with the raspberry sauce from the Dessert Taquitos on page 143, made without the chipotle chile.

RED POACHED PEARS
WITH CRÈME ANGLAISE

~~~~~~

Choosing a liquid for poaching fruit is a matter of personal taste. A simple sugar syrup is basic, but the water can be replaced with wine (white or red), a liqueur, or even a juice such as orange or cranberry. I personally like to use red wine with pears because of the rosy color it gives to the fruit. Reducing the wine with a stick of cinnamon results in a delightful spicy syrup that can be used by itself as a sauce for the pears, or as a decorative accent with the custard sauce. It's also good over ice cream.

Serves 4

    3 cups red wine
    3 cups water
    1 cup sugar
    1 stick cinnamon
    3 shavings lemon peel
    4 ripe but firm pears, peeled, halved,
        and cored
    4 mint sprigs

Crème Anglaise
    3 egg yolks
    3 tablespoons sugar
    1 cup milk
    ½ teaspoon vanilla

1. Combine the wine, water, sugar, cinnamon, and lemon peel in a saucepan and bring to a boil. Add the pears and simmer until barely tender, about 20 minutes. Let cool in the liquid, then remove. Reduce half the liquid down to a syrup to use for decoration. (The pears can be poached several days ahead of time and refrigerated in the syrup; in this case, wait to reduce the syrup on serving day.)

2. For the crème anglaise, mix the yolks and sugar in a bowl very well. Bring the milk to a boil in a saucepan and pour it into the yolk mixture, whisking to keep the milk from scrambling the eggs. Return the mixture to the pan and cook, stirring with a spoon, until it thickens and coats the back of the spoon, but *do not let it boil*. Let cool and stir in the vanilla.

3. To serve, spoon enough crème anglaise onto each plate to cover it. Place the syrup in a condiment squeeze bottle and drizzle a spiral over the crème. Run a knife point alternately from the center out and from the edge inward to form a spiderweb pattern. Place a pear on top and add a sprig of mint for color.

BREAD PUDDING

This is a dessert for the fall or winter because it contains no fresh fruit and because it is best served warm. It works best with day-old bread; if using fresh bread, let it dry out a little after you cut the chunks.

Serves 8 to 10

2 loaves (1 pound each) French bread
1½ cups raisins
1 cup brandy
1 tablespoon butter
5 eggs
3 egg yolks
¾ cup brown sugar
⅛ teaspoon salt
1½ cups milk
2 cups cream
2 teaspoons vanilla
½ teaspoon nutmeg
½ teaspoon cinnamon

1. Cut the bread into 2-inch chunks and spread out to dry a little. In a small bowl, soak the raisins in brandy until plump, about 30 minutes.

2. Preheat the oven to 350°F. Lightly butter 10 custard cups or ramekins or a 9x13-inch baking dish and place in a deep roasting pan. Mix the eggs, yolks, and the remaining ingredients together in a large bowl. Add the bread chunks and let soak until they absorb all the liquid. Fold in the raisins (and any brandy remaining in the bowl). Spoon the mixture into the prepared custard cups, ramekins, or casserole dish. Place the pan in the oven and add hot water to come halfway up the sides of the dishes. Bake until the custard is just set, about 40 minutes. Serve warm.

SOUTHWESTERN BROILED PINEAPPLE

This fast and easy dessert is a light finish to a meal. It can also double as part of a brunch menu. Remember that any item topped with sugar needs careful attention while under the broiler.

Serves 8

1 small ripe pineapple, peeled and cut into ½-inch slices

½ cup butter
½ cup brown sugar
Dash of tequila

Place the pineapple slices on a cookie sheet with sides. Melt the butter and brown sugar together and pour over the slices. Place under the broiler until bubbly and warmed through. Sprinkle with tequila and serve at once.

CHOCOLATE MOUSSE PIE

〰〰〰〰

This is the single recipe that put me on the culinary map. During my cooking school days in San Francisco, *Bon Appétit* chose one of my chocolate desserts to feature in the December 1980 issue and included it as the cover picture. The national response was overwhelming. When we opened Café Terra Cotta in Tucson, it became our signature dessert, and it is destined to remain in that position.

Serves 12 to 16

> 1½ packages (9 ounces each) Nabisco "Famous" chocolate wafers (to yield 3 cups crumbs)
> 4 ounces unsalted butter, melted
> 1 pound bittersweet chocolate
> 4 cups cream
> ⅔ cup powdered sugar
> 2 whole eggs
> 4 eggs, separated
> 6 or 8 chocolate leaves (see Note) OR shaved chocolate curls, for garnish

1. Lightly oil the sides of a 10-inch springform pan. Grind the cookies to crumbs in a food processor or blender. Mix with the melted butter and press into the bottom and up the sides of the pan. Chill.

2. Melt the chocolate in a double boiler over hot but not boiling water. Meanwhile, whip 2 cups of the cream with ⅓ cup powdered sugar. When the chocolate is melted, remove from the heat and add the whole eggs and yolks. Mix very well, then fold in the whipped cream.

3. Beat the egg whites and fold them into the chocolate mixture. Pour into the chilled crust. Chill overnight, or at least 6 hours.

4. Whip the remaining cream and sugar and spread about half the whipped cream on top of the pie. Unmold the pie and pipe the remaining cream around the edge with a pastry bag and a star tip. Arrange the chocolate leaves on top, either overlapping in the center or randomly, or scatter a layer of chocolate curls evenly over the middle.

Note: To make chocolate leaves, choose 6 to 8 camellia or other waxy leaves. Dust the leaves with a dry paper towel, but do not wash them. Melt approximately 4 ounces bittersweet chocolate in a double boiler. Using a spoon, coat the back side of each leaf with a generous layer of chocolate. Place on a plate and chill until firm. Starting at the stem, pull the leaf away from the chocolate.

To make chocolate curls, use a vegetable peeler to pare away wide, thin slices from a large block of room-temperature bittersweet chocolate. They will curl up naturally as they come off the block.

APPENDIX

OTHER SOUTHWESTERN
RESTAURANTS

MAIL ORDER SOURCES

BIBLIOGRAPHY

OTHER SOUTHWESTERN RESTAURANTS

While I can claim to be one of the originators of contemporary southwestern cuisine in Arizona, I have not been alone. Several other chefs across the Southwest and around the country have been developing their own versions of the cuisine, and these colleagues also deserve mention. Some of their restaurants described below opened before Café Terra Cotta, some afterward, and they have all contributed to making southwestern food a major influence on the restaurant scene all across America in the 1980s and 90s.

Given the risky nature of the restaurant business (only 20 percent of all restaurants last more than 5 years), I hesitate to discuss specific restaurants only to have you find out they no longer exist. However, since I can assume that if you have this book you are interested in southwestern food, I am taking that risk. Whether or not these restaurants are still operating when you read this book, the chefs that created them deserve credit for their contributions to popularizing contemporary southwestern cuisine.

CONTEMPORARY SOUTHWESTERN — CASUAL

BABY ROUTH, DALLAS, TEXAS.

Originally opened by Stephan Pyles, one of the early advocates of southwestern cuisine, this restaurant has a well deserved national reputation. The restaurant is set in an old building and has a true casual feel.

PRESIDIO GRILL, TUCSON, ARIZONA.

One of our friendly competitors in Tucson that we refer people to when we are full. Their decor, while not southwestern, is very attractive. It is one of Tucson's more popular restaurants.

COTTONWOOD CAFÉ, BETHESDA, MARYLAND.

We were very pleasantly surprised during our first visit and came back for a second in less than a week. We found the food very similar to Café Terra Cotta. It is casual and reasonably priced.

ARIZONA 206, NEW YORK CITY.

Don't laugh about southwestern restaurants in New York. Arizona 206 has been around for a while and hasn't lost its popularity. We visit it whenever we are in New York and each time it gets better. It also has a casual café which is great when you forget to make a reservation.

MESA GRILL, NEW YORK CITY.

A relative newcomer with an up and coming chef, Bobby Flay. Great food, high energy, and a noise level worthy of New York.

CILANTRO'S, DEL MAR, CALIFORNIA.

This restaurant has perhaps a little more Mexican flavor than the others listed as contemporary southwestern. The salsa is great and they sell it up front to go.

CONTEMPORARY
SOUTHWESTERN — FINE DINING

ST. ESTÈPHE, MANHATTAN BEACH, CALIFORNIA.

This restaurant closed in 1992, but deserves mentioning as one of the pioneering new southwestern restaurants. John Sedlar built his reputation here, with small portions of exquisite food set off by some of the country's best plate presentations. He later moved to Bikini in Santa Monica, where the food was more cross-cultural than southwestern. Bikini closed briefly in 1994 and reopened as Abiquiu (see Corona Bar & Grill, below).

VINCENT GUERITHAULT ON CAMELBACK, PHOENIX, ARIZONA.

Vincent is perhaps the top chef in the country when it comes to marrying French and southwestern cuisine. It's one of our favorites and our choice for special occasions.

PIÑON GRILL, SCOTTSDALE, ARIZONA.

Hotel restaurants are not usually known for great dining experiences. The Piñon Grill at the Regal McCormick Ranch is an exception. Their food is innovative, tasty, and attractively presented.

JANOS, TUCSON, ARIZONA.

Janos Wilder opened Janos just before we opened Café Terra Cotta. The original menu, which was generally nouvelle American, has become more southwestern over the years. Janos is known in Tucson for its fine dining setting in an historical house near the Tucson Art Museum.

MANSION ON TURTLE CREEK, DALLAS, TEXAS.

This is another example of a hotel having an outstanding restaurant. Dean Fearing, also one of the pioneering southwestern chefs, presides over this very formal restaurant in a beautiful setting.

CAFÉ ANNIE, HOUSTON, TEXAS.

The unusual setting in a strip shopping center in the Post Oak area of Houston hides one of the country's truly great restaurants. Well run by Chef Robert Del Grande and his wife Mimi, this is a restaurant not to be missed. We enjoyed it so much for dinner that we made lunch reservations on the way out. Great food and service.

CONTEMPORARY
MEXICAN/NEW MEXICAN

COYOTE CAFE, SANTA FE, NEW MEXICO.

Mark Miller, another one of the pioneers of southwestern cuisine, landed in New Mexico after Fourth Street Grill and Santa Fe Bar & Grill in Berkeley, California. Mark is heavily influenced by Mexican cuisine and a true believer in super spicy food. Despite being one of the most expensive southwestern restaurants in the country (only a fixed price, 3-course menu is available at night), Coyote Cafe is very popular.

BORDER GRILL, SANTA MONICA, CALIFORNIA.

A restaurant where the decor is as fun as the top-quality food. Just off the Third Street Promenade area of Santa Monica, this very casual restaurant leans heavily on Mexican cuisine.

AUTHENTIC CAFÉ, LOS ANGELES, CALIFORNIA.

This very, very small restaurant on Melrose Avenue is about as casual as it gets, even in L.A. The food, however, is a whole lot of fun and very tasty.

CORONA BAR & GRILL AND ABIQUIU, SAN FRANCISCO, CALIFORNIA.

We were having lunch at the Corona Bar and Grill a while ago when we heard the people at the next table say, "this is just like Café Terra Cotta, but more Mexican." It was, and we usually tried to make it a lunch stop when in my favorite city. In 1994 it underwent a name and menu change. Now called Abiquiu, it has taken on a more formal style under the direction of John Sedlar.

COWBOY CUISINE

In the early 1990s, "cowboy cuisine" has expanded out of a rather narrow range (T-bone steaks, ranch beans, Texas Toast, and beer in a smoky room) to a more varied, creative, even chic style in the restaurants mentioned below. I think we will see more of this new breed in the years to come, with interesting menus, less smoke, and more wine.

RED SAGE, WASHINGTON, D.C.

Mark Miller's newest hot restaurant. The decor is not to be missed. Some Mexican influence, but less than his Santa Fe style. Cowboys never had it so good.

RIO RANCH, HOUSTON, TEXAS.

Robert Del Grande's newest venture. Food and decor are very good. Straight cowboy food.

STAR CANYON, DALLAS, TEXAS.

As of press time we haven't been able to get to Dallas to try Stephan Pyles's newest restaurant, but we hear it is a hit.

MAIL ORDER SOURCES

Most cities with sizable Hispanic populations are likely to have some stores where you can buy some or all of the chiles and other southwestern ingredients called for in this book. If you do not have a local source, try one of the following mail-order suppliers. Except as noted, all take orders by mail or telephone and offer a free catalog or price list.

CREATIVE CONDIMENTS
6166 N. Scottsdale Rd.
#610
Scottsdale, AZ 85253
(800)492-4454 (49-CHILI)

MORENO BROS.
1601 E. Olympic Blvd.
#324
Los Angeles, CA 90021
(213)614-0004

MI RANCHO
464 7th St.
Oakland, CA 94606
(510)451-2393

CASA LUCAS MARKET
2934 24th St.
San Francisco, CA 94110
(415)826-4334
Walk-in sales only.

LA PALMA MEXICATESSEN
2884 24th St.
San Francisco, CA 94110
(415)647-1500

MIDWEST IMPORTS
1121 S. Clinton
Chicago, IL 60607
(312)939-8400

BUENO FOODS
P.O. Box 293
Albuquerque, NM 87103
(505)243-2722
Call or write for selection, prices.

CASADOS FARMS
P.O. Box 852
San Juan Pueblo, NM 87566
(505)852-2433
No phone orders.

THE CHILE SHOP
109 E. Water St.
Santa Fe, NM 87501
(505)983-6080

COYOTE CAFE GENERAL STORE
132 W. Water St.
Santa Fe, NM 87501
(505)982-2454

LOS CHILEROS
P.O. Box 6215
Santa Fe, NM 87502
(505)471-6967
No phone orders.

DEAN AND DELUCA
560 Broadway
New York, NY 10012
(212)431-1691
Send $3.00 for catalog.

MERCADO LATINO
245 Baldwin Park Blvd.
City of Industry, CA 91749
(818)333-6862
Also stores in San Francisco and Union City, CA.

BIBLIOGRAPHY

Bayless, Rick, and Deann Groen Bayless. *Authentic Mexican: Regional Cooking from the Heart of Mexico*. New York: Morrow, 1987.

Kennedy, Diana. *The Cuisines of Mexico*. New York: Harper & Row, 1972.

———. *Recipes from the Regional Cooks of Mexico*. New York: Harper & Row, 1978.

Miller, Mark. *The Great Chile Book*. Berkeley: Ten Speed Press, 1991.

Quintana, Patricia. *The Taste of Mexico*. New York: Stewart, Tabori & Chang, 1986.

———, with Carol Haralson. *Mexico's Feasts of Life*. Tulsa: Council Oak Books, 1989.

Rosengarten, David, and Joshua Wesson. *Red Wine with Fish*. New York: Simon and Schuster, 1989.

INDEX

Boldface numbers indicate main entries.
Italic numbers indicate photographs.

Metric Conversion Table

Follow this chart to convert the measurements in this book to their approximate metric equivalents. The metric amounts have been rounded; the slight variations in the conversion rate will not significantly change the recipes.

Liquid and Dry Volume	Metric Equivalent
1 teaspoon	5 ml
1 tablespoon (3 teaspoons)	15 ml
¼ cup	60 ml
⅓ cup	80 ml
½ cup	125 ml
1 cup	250 ml

Weight	
1 ounce	28 grams
¼ pound	113 grams
½ pound	225 grams
1 pound	450 grams

Temperature	
°Fahrenheit	°Celsius
155	70
165	75
185	85
200	95
275	135
300	150
325	160
350	175
375	190
400	205
450	230

Linear	
1 inch	2.5 cm

Other Helpful Conversion Factors

Sugar, Rice, Flour	1 teaspoon = 10 grams
	1 cup = 220 grams
Cornstarch, Salt	1 teaspoon = 5 grams
	1 tablespoon = 15 grams

ABOUT THE AUTHOR

Donna Nordin studied classic French cooking at Le Cordon Bleu and pastry with Gaston Lenôtre, both in Paris. She has taught cooking classes throughout the U.S. and operated a catering company prior to opening her first Café Terra Cotta in Tucson in 1986. She opened a second Café Terra Cotta in Scottsdale in 1992. She also owns and operates two other restaurants in Tucson, the Tohono Chul Tea Room and Trio. Ms. Nordin was featured in the PBS television series "Great Chefs of the West," and her recipes have appeared in the series companion book *Southwest Tastes* and in numerous food magazines. This is her first cookbook.

CAFÉ TERRA COTTA

The Original Café Terra Cotta in Tucson was among the pioneering restaurants featuring new southwestern cuisine, and in 1991 Mimi Sheraton of the *New York Times* and *Condé Nast Traveler* magazine named it "one of America's 50 best restaurants." John Mariani of *Esquire* magazine placed the Scottsdale branch on his 1993 list of the "Best New Restaurants" in the nation. Both restaurants continue to receive rave reviews both locally and nationally for their flavorful, imaginative contemporary southwestern cuisine.

OTHER COOKBOOKS AVAILABLE FROM HARLOW & RATNER

CONTEMPORARY ITALIAN: FAVORITE RECIPES FROM KULETO'S ITALIAN RESTAUARANT
by Robert Helstrom

Exuberant Italian cooking with a uniquely American accent, from the chef of one of San Francisco's most popular restaurants. The recipes have been carefully adapted for the home kitchen. Hardcover, 176 pages, more than 80 color photographs by John Vaughan.

JAY HARLOW'S BEER CUISINE: A COOKBOOK FOR BEER LOVERS

Much of the world's best food goes very, very well with beer. This exuberant collection offers 78 recipes ranging from snacks and nibbles to elegant dinners for company. Includes a summary of beer history and a guide to styles of beer. Quality paperback, 132 pages, including 30 full-page color photos.

MORE VEGETABLES, PLEASE: DELICIOUS VEGETABLE SIDE DISHES FOR EVERYDAY MEALS
by Janet Fletcher

All the home cook needs to know to serve a tasty, nutritious vegetable as part of dinner every day. Includes 34 easy-to-cook vegetables and more than 200 ways to serve them, plus guides to buying, storing, cleaning, and cutting each vegetable. Quality paperback, 228 pages including 32 full-page color photos.

THE COOKING OF SINGAPORE: GREAT DISHES FROM ASIA'S CULINARY CROSSROADS
by Chris Yeo and Joyce Jue

A cook's guide to the vibrant cuisine of Singapore—a unique blend of Chinese, Malaysian, Indonesian, and Indian traditions, plus the spectacular Nonya cooking style hardly known to American cooks until now. Hardcover, 176 pages including 35 pages of color photos.

NOW YOU'RE COOKING: EVERYTHING A BEGINNER NEEDS TO KNOW TO START COOKING TODAY
by Elaine Corn

An upbeat, encouraging, information-packed guide for beginners of all ages, with 150 recipes that are simple to cook and impressive to serve. Hardcover, illustrated, two-color throughout, 320 pages.

ONCE UPON A BAGEL
by Jay Harlow

What will you eat on your bagel today? Harlow provides nearly 100 tasty possibilities, including flavored cream cheeses, home-smoked salmon, and such unusual toppings as satay-style chicken and sweet and sour eggplant. Quality paperback, illustrated, 2-color throughout, 120 pages.

EVERYBODY'S WOKKING
by Martin Yan

Companion book to the ever-popular public television series "Yan Can Cook." A 176-page quality paperback with 35 pages of stunning color photos. Everybody's favorite Chinese cook, Martin Yan makes healthful Chinese cooking simple and fun.

THE WELL-SEASONED WOK
by Martin Yan

Martin Yan explores more Chinese and Southeast Asian cooking and introduces an assortment of his own East-West dishes. Quality paperback, 192 pages including 31 full-page color photos.